LOOKING
UNTO
JESUS

STEVE FOSS

CHARISMA HOUSE

LOOKING UNTO JESUS by Steve Foss
Published by Charisma House, an imprint of Charisma Media
600 Rinehart Road, Lake Mary, Florida 32746

Visit the author's website at stevefoss.com.

Cataloging-in-Publication Data is on file with the Library of Congress.
International Standard Book Number: 978-1-63641-133-0
E-book ISBN: 978-1-63641-134-7

While the author has made every effort to provide accurate internet addresses at the time of publication, neither the publisher nor the author assumes any responsibility for errors or for changes that occur after publication. Further, the publisher does not have any control over and does not assume any responsibility for author or third-party websites or their content.

23 24 25 26 27 — 987654321
Printed in the United States of America

CONTENTS

ACKNOWLEDGMENTS

I WOULD LIKE TO express my deep gratitude to Mike Bickle from IHOPKC. His teaching on the Book of Revelation is what led me to focus on these thirty descriptions of Jesus. His passion for the revelation of Jesus is contagious and had a profound effect on this journey you are about to go on with me in *Looking Unto Jesus: 30 Days of Transformation*.

I also want to thank Travis McCarn for his many hours of labor in helping me with the editing and review of this book. Your passion for the truth of God's Word is an inspiration to many. I greatly appreciate your partnership in ministry and how mightily the Holy Spirit uses you. My prayer for you as my Timothy is that God will expand your ministry and use you in greater ways than He has used me.

Introduction
THE SPIRIT OF REVELATION

"I SEE IT; I see it; I see it," I cried out, with tears bursting from my eyes as I fell to my knees. I was having an open vision. I suddenly found myself standing in a vast, seemingly endless expanse. I could not see the room or anything around me, but I saw these words from Ephesians 1:17 hovering in the air: "That the God of our Lord Jesus Christ, the Father of glory, may give you the Spirit of wisdom and revelation in the knowledge of Him" (MEV).

The most amazing blue-white light shone forth and filled the expanse. It was not from behind the words or in front of the words, but from within the very words themselves. I knew it was the shekinah glory of God. As I beheld this awesome sight, crying out "I see it; I see it," I heard the voice of the Lord speak, and it sounded like thunder.

God said, "Through My Word you'll see Me."

I had been listening to a cassette recording of Dr. Morris Cerullo preaching the first message from his Unity in the Spirit conference. I was in my rented mobile home on this cool California night in early March 1987. Dr. Cerullo preached on Ephesians 1:17–18 for about six minutes, and something triggered inside of me. I knew there was a much deeper truth than what I perceived thus far, so I rewound the tape and listened to that section over and over again for two hours. Each time, as I prayed over the words Dr. Cerullo preached, I caught a glimpse that it was possible to see Jesus with the eyes of my heart.

My roommate came home, and I tried three times to tell him what I was feeling and seeing. Each time as I tried to explain the revelation, I became overwhelmed and could not speak for about five minutes. I stood in front of him with my face buried in my Bible, speechless. The third time, as I felt myself becoming overwhelmed, I was suddenly having an open vision. I no longer saw my roommate or the room where we stood. I was in a heavenly place.

This encounter was the defining experience of my life. This divine impartation of the Spirit of wisdom and revelation began my lifelong journey of wanting to discover and uncover the unsearchable riches of Christ. My heart's cry became "to know Him, and the power of His resurrection, and the fellowship of His sufferings, being conformed to His death" (Phil. 3:10, MEV).

I have traveled millions of miles to countless nations and preached to millions of people around the world. I have discovered one overriding truth. This truth will transform your life into the most amazing, victorious, exciting, and ever-increasing adventure of all lifetimes. This truth will keep a fiery passion burning in your heart for Jesus no matter how difficult your circumstances are. This truth will fascinate your heart beyond anything you could ever experience in this natural life.

The truth I discovered in this life-changing experience in March 1987 was this: nothing will transform the human heart like the revelation of the person of Jesus Christ.

We have countless books and teachings on thirty steps to victory, eighteen steps to faith, twelve steps to overcoming addictions, and on and on. Some of these methods have helped people in certain areas of their lives, but nothing can even come close to the transformation of the human heart that takes place through the pure, deep, and intimate revelation knowledge of the person of Jesus.

> And all of us, as with unveiled face, [because we] continued to behold [in the Word of God] as in a mirror the glory of the Lord, are constantly being transfigured into His very own image in ever increasing splendor and from one degree of glory to another; [for this comes] from the Lord [Who is] the Spirit.
>
> —2 Corinthians 3:18, AMPC

As we continually behold Jesus in the Word of God, we are transformed into His likeness. Only when we see Him as He is do we become like Him. This is our eternal destiny. "We know that when He is revealed, we shall be like Him, for we shall see Him as He is" (1 John 3:2). "For those whom He foreknew, He predestined to be conformed to the image of His Son" (Rom. 8:29, MEV).

Paul in his letter to the Ephesians was writing to and praying for the most spiritually mature people of his day. He prayed that God would grant them a special new anointing of "wisdom and revelation [of insight into mysteries and secrets] in the [deep and intimate] knowledge of Him" (Eph. 1:17, AMPC).

He said this would happen "by having the eyes of your heart flooded with light" (Eph. 1:18, AMPC). This is the light "of the knowledge of the majesty and glory of God [as it is manifest in the Person and is revealed] in the face of Jesus Christ (the Messiah)" (2 Cor. 4:6, AMPC).

Only the light of the knowledge of the glory of God as revealed in the face of Jesus flooding our hearts and minds will transform us into His image. It is the revelation knowledge of Him that changes everything.

My life's journey has been this one thing: that I may know Him. That journey has led me to what may be the most significant chapter in the Bible because it gives more understanding of the person of Jesus Christ than any other chapter.

This one chapter has more than two dozen descriptions of Jesus. Each description is loaded with incredible revelation of who Jesus is and what He is focused on. These descriptions reveal His character, His nature, His authority, and His kingdom.

This portion of Scripture is Revelation chapter 1.

The first five words of Revelation reveal what the entire book is about: the Revelation of Jesus Christ. The book is mostly about revealing who Jesus is and what He will do to fulfill His eternal plan. The next few words give us incredible insight: "which God gave Him to show His servants" (Rev. 1:1).

God the Father gave the instructions for Jesus to show His servants these revelations. Through the Book of Revelation the Father provided an end-time generation the revelations they would need to stand victorious in the most intense time the world would ever experience. God has planned that in the last days He will release the greatest revelation of Jesus Christ that the world has ever known.

Paul in Ephesians told us that the time is coming when God will reveal more of Himself and His plans than at any other time in history. He called that period the maturity of the times and the climax of the ages. In Revelation, God says that in the last days He will unveil the great mysteries of Jesus in an unprecedented dimension.

> Making known to us the mystery (secret) of His will (of His plan, of His purpose). [And it is this:] In accordance with His good pleasure (His merciful intention) which He had previously purposed and set forth in Him, [He planned] for the maturity of the times and the climax of the ages to unify all things and head them up and consummate them in Christ, [both] things in heaven and things on the earth.
>
> —EPHESIANS 1:9–10, AMPC

The Father knew that the only thing that would empower an end-time people to stand in the face of wickedness would be the greatest revelation of His Son Jesus that the world has ever known. We are in those days, the maturity of the times and the climax of the ages. We are in the last days. I don't know how long it will last—ten years, twenty, fifty, or more—but this is it.

We are privileged to live in a day when God is opening His Word like never before to those who hunger and thirst for Him. Over the next thirty days we are going to explore these amazing revelations of who Jesus is and what He is focused on.

These descriptions are so profound that you could write volumes of books on each one. My prayer is that as we take a glimpse into these transformative revelations, you will start a lifelong journey to search out the unsearchable riches of Christ and be wholly filled and flooded with God.

I encourage you to read one chapter each day for the next thirty days. Meditate on it, pray over it, talk about it, and let each revelation sink deep into your spirit. Some may want to read it quickly, but I encourage you not to. Let the marinating of God's Word and the revelation of who He is penetrate your innermost being. This is not a sprint; this is a marathon. Take your time and behold the glory of the One who loves you.

Nothing transforms the human heart like the revelation of the person of Jesus Christ.

Let's begin our thirty days of transformation.

Day 1
THE ESSENCE OF GOD

Grace to you and peace from Him who is
and who was and who is to come.
—REVELATION 1:4

W HEN THE APOSTLE John begins the Book of Revelation,
he invokes a powerful apostolic declaration that grace
and peace may come to you and be upon you. This is not just a
greeting but a powerful revelation of how we can grow in the favor
of God and access the power of God for everything we need for
life and godliness.

> Grace and peace be multiplied to you in the knowledge of
> God and of Jesus our Lord, as His divine power has given
> to us all things that pertain to life and godliness, through
> the knowledge of Him who called us by glory and virtue.
> —2 PETER 1:2–3

John is about to reveal the amazing descriptions of Jesus in
Revelation 1 that will transform our lives to enable us to walk in
the fullness of the power we need to overcome every assault of the
enemy. We see that grace and peace are multiplied in our lives
through the revelation knowledge of God and Jesus. God's divine
power is made manifest in our lives in direct proportion to the
revelation knowledge of Him that we have received. Through the
knowledge of Him we access the divine power of God for everything we need to live a godly life.

The grace of God, which is God's unmerited favor, and the
peace of God, which is harmony and tranquility and speaks of our
being "at one again" with God, will be multiplied to you through
the revelation of who He is.[1] As you come to know and understand

God, you will gain favor with Him, and your harmony and oneness with God will be multiplied.

I find it powerful that Revelation begins with this declaration,
and it repeats greetings and declarations found earlier in the Old
Testament: God is always the same, has always existed, and never
changes: "For I am the LORD, I do not change; therefore you are
not consumed, O sons of Jacob" (Mal. 3:6).

To understand Jesus, it is vitally important to realize that God
never changes. We are reminded in the Book of Hebrews that
"Jesus Christ is the same yesterday, today, and forever" (Heb. 13:8).
If you listen to some modern teachings on grace, you could almost
think Jesus came to deliver us from His mean Father. Many
people have the false understanding that the Father is the God of
wrath, and Jesus is the God of mercy. Many Christians avoid the
Old Testament because they think it is just law and bondage. They
think God has changed.

God has not changed. The covenant has changed, but God and
His nature have not changed.

This also points us to the mystery of the Trinity—the Father,
the Son, and the Holy Spirit, the one God fully self-existent in
three persons. Since God is Three in One, this description applies
to the entirety of the Godhead.

Jesus is revealed from the beginning of Scripture to the end.
He is in every book, every story, and every commandment. Jesus'
nature, character, authority, and kingdom are revealed throughout
Scripture. Jesus is the same as He has always been.

As we study these descriptions of Jesus in Revelation, we will
look back into the Old Testament to see what they reveal to us.
God never changes. This knowledge gives us understanding and
confidence and allows us to stand strong in an ever-changing
world. He alone is our rock and our stability.

> Wisdom and knowledge will be the stability of your
> times, and the strength of salvation; the fear of the LORD
> is His treasure.
>
> —ISAIAH 33:6

The word for *stability* means "the quality of being steady, securely or immovably fixed in place."[2] The wisdom and revelation knowledge of God empowers you to be immovably fixed in place. You will be secure and steady. You will be at peace because no matter what is happening around you, your eyes will be fixed on Him, and you will not be moved.

Paul was able to not lose hope even when he was left for dead because he understood that God never changes. He reminded the Corinthians of the intense persecution that he endured not knowing if he would live.

> For we do not want you to be ignorant, brethren, of our trouble which came to us in Asia: that we were burdened beyond measure, above strength, so that we despaired even of life. Yes, we had the sentence of death in ourselves, that we should not trust in ourselves but in God who raises the dead, who delivered us from so great a death, and does deliver us; in whom we trust that He will still deliver us.
>
> —2 Corinthians 1:8–10

Paul rested in Christ even when he did not know what was going to happen because he knew that God had delivered him in the past, and he could trust that God would deliver him in the future. He knew that God would raise him from the dead if his work was not completed. Paul was able to pass along this unshakable faith to the Christians at Corinth because he spoke from experience.

So let us now come into the understanding of the God "who is and who was and who is to come."

The God *Who Is*

"And God said to Moses, 'I Am Who I Am'" (Exod. 3:14, mev). God is saying what we might think is obvious, but this is the foundation of everything, the truth that God exists. There is a personal, all-powerful Creator of everything who exists. The awareness that

God Almighty is ever present and is an absolute reality, when believed, will impact every part of our lives.

Many say they believe in God, but they live like He doesn't really exist. Modern scientific thinking is always trying to explain existence without God. We relegate Jesus to a religious belief system, but in doing so we forget that He is the God who is. God is saying, "I am everything, everywhere, all the time. I am the source of all life, all power, all creation, and all that is seen and unseen." "All things were created through Him, and without Him nothing was created that was created" (John 1:3, MEV).

God is saying, "I Am Who I Am, not who humans want Me to be. I am not like you. I am infinitely above and beyond you."

> "For My thoughts are not your thoughts, nor are your ways My ways," says the LORD. "For as the heavens are higher than the earth, so are My ways higher than your ways, and My thoughts than your thoughts."
>
> —ISAIAH 55:8–9

We begin our journey with the realization that Jesus is who He is and not necessarily who we think He is. We must clear our minds of all our preconceived ideas and ask the Holy Spirit to reveal to us who Jesus really is. When we see Jesus as He really is, we will understand what He does. Only then will we be able to walk in perfect peace.

THE GOD *WHO WAS*

Jesus has always been. He is "the Beginning of the creation of God" (Rev. 3:14). "In the beginning was the Word, and the Word was with God, and the Word was God. He was in the beginning with God" (John 1:1–2).

The living creatures and elders around the throne worshipped God, saying, "You are worthy, O Lord, to receive glory and honor and power; for You created all things, and by Your will they exist and were created" (Rev. 4:11).

Moses declares in Psalm 90:2, "Before the mountains were

brought forth, or ever You had formed the earth and the world, even from everlasting to everlasting, You are God."

God is eternally self-existent. He has no beginning and no ending. He has always been and always will be. Everything that is was created by Him, for Him, and through Him. The focus on the eternal nature of God gives us absolute confidence that His plans and purposes will be fulfilled. He who always was and created all things also created us for a divine plan and purpose.

Ephesians 1:4–5 states, "He chose us in Him before the foundation of the world, that we should be holy and without blame before Him in love, having predestined us to adoption as sons by Jesus Christ to Himself, according to the good pleasure of His will."

God inhabits eternity. He fills all space and time with Himself. The One who is and was and always will be longs to dwell with you and me.

> For thus says the High and Lofty One who inhabits eternity, whose name is Holy: "I dwell in the high and holy place, with him who has a contrite and humble spirit, to revive the spirit of the humble, and to revive the heart of the contrite ones."
>
> —Isaiah 57:15

THE GOD *WHO IS TO COME*

These descriptions are preparing a people for the most intense season the world will ever experience. These truths will give us the strength we need to overcome every fiery dart of the evil one. John begins the Book of Revelation by drawing our attention to these three truths: that God is and was and is to come. God is the holy Trinity, three persons in one: God the Father, Jesus the Son, and the Holy Spirit. God through Jesus is everywhere and is all things. Jesus has always been, and all things were created by and through Him. Jesus is coming again, so we can rest in confident hope of our final salvation from this present darkness.

Let not your heart be troubled; you believe in God, believe
also in Me. In My Father's house are many mansions; if it
were not so, I would have told you. I go to prepare a place
for you. And if I go and prepare a place for you, I will
come again and receive you to Myself; that where I am,
there you may be also.
—JOHN 14:1–3

Do not be troubled by what you are going through! Jesus is
coming to take you to be with Him forever.

God spoke a prophetic word to me a few years ago. He said,
"Only a focus on eternity and the second coming of Christ will protect your minds from the onslaught of the enemy that is coming."
We must focus strongly and consistently on Jesus, who is coming
again. This focus on the God *who is to come* will empower us not
to fear.

Behold, I tell you a mystery: We shall not all sleep, but we
shall all be changed—in a moment, in the twinkling of
an eye, at the last trumpet. For the trumpet will sound,
and the dead will be raised incorruptible, and we shall
be changed. For this corruptible must put on incorruption, and this mortal must put on immortality. So when
this corruptible has put on incorruption, and this mortal
has put on immortality, then shall be brought to pass the
saying that is written: *"Death is swallowed up in victory."*

"O Death, where is your sting? O Hades, where is your
victory?"
—1 CORINTHIANS 15:51–55, EMPHASIS ADDED

For the Lord Himself will descend from heaven with
a shout, with the voice of an archangel, and with the
trumpet of God. And the dead in Christ will rise first.
Then we who are alive and remain shall be caught up
together with them in the clouds to meet the Lord in the
air. And thus we shall always be with the Lord. Therefore
comfort one another with these words.
—1 THESSALONIANS 4:16–18

Paul commands us to comfort one another with these words about the second coming of Christ. I have asked many people recently whether they are hearing messages preached about the second coming of Christ. Most say rarely, if ever. This is a great danger. Without a proper focus on who Jesus is and what He is focused on, we will be easily overwhelmed by the days ahead. God the Father gave Jesus a command to reveal to us these descriptions of Himself in the Book of Revelation to empower us to walk in total victory.

The purpose of our journey is to look unto Jesus and see Him as the One "who is and who was and who is to come" (Rev. 1:4). Jesus is "the same yesterday, today, and forever" (Heb. 13:8). Wake up each morning and spend a few minutes meditating on the reality that God *is*. He is the I Am who has always been and always will be. He fills the universe with Himself, and He longs to spend eternity with you.

Prayer

Father, fill me with the knowledge of Your eternal nature, for I declare You are the one and only true God who is, who was, and who is to come. You have always been, and You will always be. You are the same. You have never changed; therefore, I can fully trust in You. You and You alone inhabit eternity and have set Your gaze upon me this day. May my eyes be upon You always, I pray, in the name of Your holy Son, Jesus. Amen.

Day 2
THE SEVEN SPIRITS OF GOD

...and from the seven Spirits who are before His throne.
—REVELATION 1:4

G OD IS TOTALLY self-existent as Three in One: the Father, the Son, and the Holy Spirit. Together they form the holy Trinity, the essence of God, but they are three distinct persons. The mystery of the Godhead is hard for us to comprehend. God is not three gods in agreement with one another. There is only one God. As Deuteronomy 6:4 proclaims, "Hear, O Israel: The LORD our God, the LORD is one!"

The Godhead is more than three personalities or expressions of God. The members of the Trinity are in substance or essence One yet individually distinct.

"There are various gifts, but the same Spirit. There are differences of administrations, but the same Lord. There are various operations, but it is the same God who operates all of them in all people" (1 Cor. 12:4–6, MEV). We see in this verse the Holy Spirit, the Lord Jesus, and the Father God. The Father is the operator of the gifts, Jesus is the administrator of the gifts, and the Holy Spirit divides and distributes the gifts among the saints.

So in character, nature, and being they are One, but in function there are distinctions. All three are involved in the release and manifestation of the gifts of the Spirit, but all three have distinct roles.

John begins in Revelation by exposing the truth of the Trinity while also revealing incredible foundational truths. God who is, who was, and who is to come is the foundation of all truth. This is the reality of the eternal nature and existence of God.

The second truth is the seven manifestations of the Spirit of God that were upon Jesus:

> The Spirit of the LORD shall rest upon Him, the Spirit of wisdom and understanding, the Spirit of counsel and might, the Spirit of knowledge and of the fear of the LORD.
>
> —ISAIAH 11:2

The number seven speaks of completeness and perfection. The fullness of the manifestation of the Holy Spirit was upon Jesus while He walked on the earth. It is the same Holy Spirit that Jesus promised to send to us. That Spirit would anoint us and live within us. When we see how Jesus walked in total victory, we discover how we can live and walk in total victory. The same Holy Spirit that anointed and empowered Jesus is the Holy Spirit that you and I have.

In Revelation 5, when John saw the scroll that no one was worthy to open, he then saw an image of Jesus. "I saw a Lamb in the midst of the throne and of the four living creatures, and in the midst of the elders, standing as though it had been slain, having seven horns and seven eyes, which are the seven Spirits of God, sent out into all the earth" (Rev. 5:6, MEV).

Jesus appeared as a Lamb slain, which shows Him as the worthy sacrifice to take away our sins. John also saw seven horns, "that is, *perfect might*." The number seven is "symbolizing *perfection*," and the horns are symbolizing might.[1] He also sees seven eyes. The eyes "symbolize His all-watchful and wise providence for His Church, and against her foes."[2] The seven manifestations of the Holy Spirit that were upon Jesus have been sent out into the earth with full power and wisdom to be expressed through the church in the earth.

Then Jesus takes the scroll to unleash the end-time events onto the earth. The greatest manifestation of the Holy Spirit the world will ever see will be released at the end of the age.

> And it shall come to pass in the last days, says God, that I
> will pour out of My Spirit on all flesh; your sons and your
> daughters shall prophesy, your young men shall see visions,
> your old men shall dream dreams. And on My men-
> servants and on My maidservants I will pour out My Spirit
> in those days; and they shall prophesy. I will show won-
> ders in heaven above and signs in the earth beneath: blood
> and fire and vapor of smoke. The sun shall be turned into
> darkness, and the moon into blood, before the coming of
> the great and awesome day of the LORD. And it shall come
> to pass that whoever calls on the name of the LORD shall
> be saved.
>
> —ACTS 2:17–21

In the last days the greatest manifestation of the Holy Spirit
will happen. A prophetic anointing will be released. Signs and
wonders in the heavens and on the earth will release the power
and glory of God through grace to His people and judgment on
the earth. The prophet Malachi says this will happen "…before the
coming of the great and dreaded day of the LORD" (Mal. 4:5, MEV).

The day of the Lord and His wrath does not happen until the
sixth seal. "I watched as He opened the sixth seal. And suddenly
there was a great earthquake. The sun became black, like sack-
cloth made from goat hair, and the moon became like blood….For
the great day of His wrath has come. Who is able to withstand it?"
(Rev. 6:12, 17, MEV).

Finally, this fullness of the release of the seven Spirits of God
will result in the greatest harvest of souls the world has ever seen.
"And whoever calls on the name of the LORD shall be saved" (Acts
2:21, MEV).

SEVEN MANIFESTATIONS OF THE HOLY SPIRIT

The seven manifestations of the Holy Spirit—what Revelation 1:4
calls the "seven Spirits who are before His throne"—are going to
increase exponentially as the end of days approaches. I believe we

are in the beginnings of those days. The seven manifestations of
the Holy Spirit listed in Isaiah 11:2 are as follows.

1. "The Spirit of the LORD shall rest upon Him."

The word *rest* means to "settle down and remain."[3] "Then John
bore witness, saying, 'I saw the Spirit descending from heaven
like a dove, and it remained on Him'" (John 1:32, MEV). The Holy
Spirit was already *in* Jesus, but now a new power and manifestation came to *rest on* Jesus. This unique resting of the power from
heaven is what gave Jesus the ability to do the work that the Father
gave Him.

We too have the Holy Spirit in us if we are born again. However,
we also need the Holy Spirit to rest on us. Throughout history this
resting has been called many things, from the second blessing to
the baptism of the Holy Spirit. It is much greater than the release
of a particular gift of the Spirit, such as speaking in tongues. This
indwelling of the Spirit is a resting and remaining of God's power
continually on one's life.

2. The Spirit of wisdom

Wisdom is "the capacity to understand and so have skill in
living."[4] This supernatural wisdom gives us the capacity to understand the degree to which we are skilled in doing the works of God.
Jesus did not function on the earth in His own divine wisdom. He
depended on the same Holy Spirit wisdom that we have access to.

The wisdom of God is not from the intellectual minds of men.
When God told Moses to build the tabernacle, God anointed
Bezalel to do the work. "I have filled him with the Spirit of God
in wisdom, in understanding, in knowledge, and in all manner of
craftsmanship" (Exod. 31:3, MEV).

Jesus was anointed with the supernatural wisdom to be skilled
in doing the works of God. Only the wisdom of God can properly build God's house, and in New Testament Christianity *we* are
God's house. We too must receive this same supernatural wisdom,
and the Bible tells us how. "If any of you lacks wisdom, let him ask

of God, who gives to all liberally and without reproach, and it will be given to him" (Jas. 1:5).

3. The Spirit of understanding

Understanding means "insight, discernment...to be given a revelation as well as its meaning."[5] I like to call this one the Spirit of revelation. This is a supernatural anointing of God that gives us insight into the mysteries and secrets of God. This is more than book knowledge; rather, it is the power to understand to the point that it becomes an experience.

Paul prayed that wisdom and revelation would be given to the Ephesians. He was praying for people who were already born again but who wanted this manifestation of the Holy Spirit to rest on them.

> [For I always pray to] the God of our Lord Jesus Christ, the Father of glory, that He may grant you a spirit of wisdom and revelation [of insight into mysteries and secrets] in the [deep and intimate] knowledge of Him.
> —EPHESIANS 1:17, AMPC

4. The Spirit of counsel

Counsel means "the act of telling someone what they should do based on a plan."[6] Jesus walked under the supernatural counsel of His Father as given by the Holy Spirit. This is revealed in the Book of John: "For I have not spoken on My own authority; but the Father who sent Me gave Me a command, what I should say and what I should speak" (John 12:49, MEV). "So Jesus said to them, 'When you lift up the Son of Man, then you will know that I am He, and I do nothing of Myself. But I speak these things as My Father taught Me'" (John 8:28, MEV).

Jesus always operated under the divine instructions of the Father according to the Father's plan. Jesus promised us that "when the Spirit of truth comes, He will guide you into all truth. For He will not speak on His own authority. But He will speak whatever He hears, and He will tell you things that are to come" (John 16:13, MEV).

The Spirit of counsel gives the specific strategies and instructions needed to fulfill the plans and purposes of God.

5. The Spirit of might

Might means "power, strength…victory, i.e., a soldier strong and capable to defeat an enemy."[7]

The Spirit of might is a supernatural power over all the power of the enemy. This is the power to overcome. Jesus said, "I have told you these things so that in Me you may have peace. In the world you will have tribulation. But be of good cheer. I have overcome the world" (John 16:33, MEV).

Jesus overcame the world and defeated the enemy through the Spirit of might. The power for victory that flows from the Holy Spirit cannot be underestimated. God's power of might is far beyond all the power of the enemy. This power is only going to increase as the day of the Lord approaches. The last-days church is going to be filled with supernatural might. Speaking of the end times, God says, "The one who stumbles among them will be as David on that day. And the house of David will be like God, like the angel of the LORD going out before them" (Zech. 12:8, MEV). The weakest and feeblest among God's people will be as powerful as King David. Let that sink into your spirit.

6. The Spirit of knowledge

In this usage, *knowledge* means a "focus on moral qualities and its application, i.e., information of a person, with a strong implication of relationship to that person."[8]

This anointing for knowledge strongly applies to knowing God intimately and personally. At the end of Paul's life, he declared that he wanted "to know Him, and the power of His resurrection, and the fellowship of His sufferings, being conformed to His death" (Phil. 3:10, MEV). As the return of Christ approaches, we will see a greater manifestation of an intimate personal knowledge of God.

"But let him who glories glory in this, that he understands and knows Me" (Jer. 9:24, MEV). We have entered the days when we will know Jesus in greater measure than any generation before us.

This intimate personal knowledge of God will empower us to be the final and greatest witness of Jesus to the world, and then the end shall come.

7. The Spirit of the fear of the Lord

Fear in this usage is defined as "a feeling of profound respect for someone...conceived of as fear."[9] It speaks of an overwhelming awe of God to the point of terror.

> The angel of the LORD encamps all around those who fear Him, and delivers them....Oh, fear the LORD, you His saints! There is no want to those who fear Him.
> —PSALM 34:7, 9

The fear of the Lord is returning to the church, and that is a good thing. If Jesus was anointed with the Spirit of the fear of the Lord, we should be too. This awe of God is required to be close to God.

> This is what the LORD spoke, saying: "By those who come near Me I must be regarded as holy; and before all the people I must be glorified."
> —LEVITICUS 10:3

These seven Spirits of God are the seven manifestations of the Holy Spirit that were upon the life of Jesus. Likewise, these seven Spirits will be released in the last days at full measure throughout the church. The descriptions of Jesus in Revelation chapter 1 are there for a reason: to prepare a people for the most intense season the world will ever experience. As we look unto Jesus, we are changed into His image and filled with His strength.

As we see how Jesus lived on this earth by the same power of the Holy Spirit that He has now made available to us, we can stand strong in confidence that if Jesus overcame, we too can overcome. It is our prayer that the Holy Spirit will rest upon us as it releases the fullness of these seven manifestations upon our lives.

Prayer

Father, fill me today with the same seven manifestations of the Holy Spirit that were upon Jesus. May the Holy Spirit rest upon me in fullness. I ask and receive Your wisdom and understanding to follow You wholeheartedly; Your counsel and might to fulfill Your kingdom purposes in and through my life; and knowledge with the fear of the Lord to engage with You with deep awe and ever-increasing intimacy. I believe and I receive in the name of Your holy Son, Jesus. Amen.

Day 3
THE POWER OF
JESUS' NAME

"And from Jesus Christ," the One given "the
name which is above every name."
—REVELATION 1:5; PHILIPPIANS 2:9

IF YOU ASK most Christians if they know Jesus, they will respond
with a confident yes. Yet to what extent do we see Him? Is our
view of Him accurate and correct? Imagine the apostle John. He
walked with Jesus for more than three years. He saw the visible
glory of Jesus on the Mount of Transfiguration (and he saw Elijah
and Moses). He saw Jesus walk on water. He was the closest one to
Jesus. He was the only disciple at the cross during the crucifixion.
He saw Jesus after He was raised from the dead, and then he saw
Jesus ascend into the clouds.

Have any of us had anything even close to this kind of experience or encounter with Jesus? Even after all this, when Jesus
reveals Himself to John in Revelation 1, John is so overwhelmed
by this revelation that he falls to the ground as a dead man.

> Then I turned to see the voice that spoke with me. And
> having turned I saw seven golden lampstands, and in
> the midst of the seven lampstands One like the Son of
> Man, clothed with a garment down to the feet and girded
> about the chest with a golden band. His head and hair
> were white like wool, as white as snow, and His eyes like
> a flame of fire; His feet were like fine brass, as if refined
> in a furnace, and His voice as the sound of many waters;
> He had in His right hand seven stars, out of His mouth
> went a sharp two-edged sword, and His countenance was
> like the sun shining in its strength. And when I saw Him,
> I fell at His feet as dead.
>
> —REVELATION 1:12–17

This revelation was so far superior to anything John had known before that his body could not handle it. This is the revelation that God wants to give to you and me—a fresh, new, overwhelming revelation—so that we are fully prepared to face any battle, crisis, or persecution that may come our way and are fully equipped to fulfill our eternal destiny in Christ.

The eternal One who is, who was, who is to come, and upon whom rests the seven manifestations of the Holy Spirit, has the name that is above every other name—Jesus. It all begins with the name of Jesus, Yeshua, which means "God saves."[1]

A name throughout history speaks of nature, character, authority, and destiny. Jesus wasn't given just any name; He has been given the highest of all names.

> Therefore God also has highly exalted Him and given Him the name which is above every name, that at the name of Jesus every knee should bow, of those in heaven, and of those on earth, and of those under the earth, and that every tongue should confess that Jesus Christ is Lord, to the glory of God the Father.
>
> —PHILIPPIANS 2:9–11

If we want to understand the power of the name of Jesus, we must understand its importance and preeminence in all things. Everything that ever was, is, or is to come is all about Him and all for His name's sake. There is only One who is worthy. There is only One who paid the price for sin. There is only One who rose from the dead and conquered death, hell, and the grave.

Our western Christianity is predominately focused on who we are "in Christ" and what He will do for us. This was *never* the focus of Jesus and the Father. If we want to see Jesus as He is, then we *must* understand this truth. Christianity is not about you or me. Instead, it is all for His name's sake.

JESUS—IT IS FOR HIS NAME'S SAKE

In this section, we will look more closely at five aspects of the power and purpose of Jesus' name.

1. He forgives you for His name's sake.

> I, even I, am He who blots out your transgressions for My own sake; and I will not remember your sins.
>
> —ISAIAH 43:25

2. He cleanses you and gives you His Spirit for His name's sake.

> I do not do this for your sake, O house of Israel, but for My holy name's sake....Then I will sprinkle clean water on you, and you shall be clean; I will cleanse you from all your filthiness and from all your idols. I will give you a new heart and put a new spirit within you; I will take the heart of stone out of your flesh and give you a heart of flesh. I will put My Spirit within you and cause you to walk in My statutes, and you will keep My judgments and do them.
>
> —EZEKIEL 36:22, 25–27

3. He saved you for His name's sake.

> Nevertheless He saved them for His name's sake, that He might make His mighty power known.
>
> —PSALM 106:8

4. All that we do is for the glory of God's name.

> Help us, O God of our salvation, for the glory of Your name; and deliver us, and provide atonement for our sins, for Your name's sake! Why should the nations say, "Where is their God?"
>
> —PSALM 79:9–10

5. He restrains judgment for His name's sake.

> For My name's sake I will defer My anger, and for My praise I will restrain it from you, so that I do not cut you off. Behold, I have refined you, but not as silver; I have tested you in the furnace of affliction. For My own sake, for My own sake, I will do it; for how should My name be profaned? And I will not give My glory to another.
>
> —ISAIAH 48:9–11

Everything always has been and always will be for Jesus' name's sake and for His glory. This is an eternal truth. We are the incredible recipients of His love, mercy, grace, kindness, patience, and every spiritual blessing, but it is all for His name's sake and glory.

JESUS—IT IS FOR HIS GLORY

When Paul wrote to the Corinthian Christians, he focused on this amazing truth—that it is all for Jesus and His glory.

> Therefore, whether you eat or drink, or whatever you do, do all to the glory of God.
>
> —1 CORINTHIANS 10:31

Everything that God has ever done and will ever do is for His name's sake and under His authority. All things are done for His glory, His honor, His praise, and His good pleasure. He alone is worthy.

In the revelation of Jesus' name, we see His absolute authority over everything that is named. Jesus is "far above all principalities, and power, and might, and dominion, and every name that is named, not only in this age but also in that which is to come" (Eph. 1:21, MEV).

Jesus came to fulfill the will of His Father. He came to reveal His Father to the world. Jesus' driving purpose was to reveal the Father's name to us. He came to reveal God's character, nature, authority, and kingdom to mankind through His Father's name.

I have glorified You on the earth. I have finished the
work which You have given Me to do....I have manifested
Your name to the men whom You have given Me out of
the world....Now I am no longer in the world, but these
are in the world, and I come to You. Holy Father, keep
through Your name those whom You have given Me, that
they may be one as We are. While I was with them in the
world, I kept them in Your name....And I have declared
to them Your name, and will declare it, that the love with
which You loved Me may be in them, and I in them.
—JOHN 17:4, 6, 11–12, 26

Jesus says in His final prayer that He finished the work God
gave Him. And what was that work? He glorified His Father on
the earth and manifested His name. He then prays for us that the
Father will keep us "in His name," just as He kept them in His
name while He was with His disciples.

Then in verse 26, the very end of Jesus' final prayer, He says,
"I have declared to them Your name, and will declare it." Jesus
is saying that He has revealed and will continue to reveal His
Father's name—His character, nature, authority, plans, and purpose—to the believers.

As this revelation of the name of God grows, an amazing thing
takes place: Jesus prays that "the love with which You loved Me
may be in them, and I in them."

Jesus is saying that as we continue to grow in the revelation of
the name of God, the love of God is imparted to us. Only as we
focus on Jesus and who He is can we receive and possess the agape
love of God. This love is unconditional and freely given by God's
grace.

JESUS—IT IS ABOUT HIS AUTHORITY

Because Jesus was faithful to reveal the name of the Father, He was
given the name above every other name. Then Jesus went to His
disciples and commissioned them to go in His name. "Then Jesus

came and spoke to them, saying, 'All authority has been given to Me in heaven and on earth. Go therefore'" (Matt. 28:18–19, MEV).

The name of Jesus—or in other words, the revelation of His character, nature, authority, and kingdom—has been given to us so we can gain access to the Father. We have the right to use the authority of His name as we obey His commands. "If you remain in Me, and My words remain in you, you will ask whatever you desire, and it shall be done for you" (John 15:7, MEV).

Jesus said, "I will do whatever you ask in My name, that the Father may be glorified in the Son. If you ask anything in My name, I will do it" (John 14:13–14, MEV).

If you ask the Father anything, and come to the Father in obedience to the revelation of His character, nature, authority, and kingdom, He will give it to you.

Jesus has all power and authority, so if you ask the Father while yielding to His power and authority, you will receive what you ask for. This is what it means to pray in the name of Jesus. It is to pray from the revelation of His name and in submission to His power, authority, character, and kingdom.

When Jesus taught His disciples to pray, He brought forth this same revelation.

> Our Father in heaven, hallowed be Your name. Your kingdom [authority] come. Your will be done [for Your name's sake and for Your glory] on earth as it is in heaven.
> —MATTHEW 6:9–10

Whatever we ask the Father in Jesus' name, for His name's sake, for His glory, and under His authority, we are guaranteed to receive it. There is power in the name of Jesus.

Prayer

Father, in the name of Your Son Jesus, I humble myself and empty myself of my preconceived ideas. Anoint me with supernatural understanding to see Jesus as He is. I confess that all things are done for Your name's sake and for Your glory. I agree that none is worthy but You. I know that because of Your loving-kindness, mercy, and grace, I have received salvation and every spiritual blessing in heavenly places.

Forgive me for making things so much about me. I am Yours. I was created for Your good pleasure. I was fashioned to show forth Your praises and to bring glory to Your name. I thank You that You have looked down from heaven and have chosen to dwell with the humble. I humble myself before You and look unto You. Jesus, my eyes are upon You. Help me see You as You are that I may glorify Your name.

Day 4
SIX PURPOSES OF CHRIST

Grace to you and peace from Him who is and who was and who is to come, and from the seven Spirits who are before His throne, and from Jesus Christ.

—REVELATION 1:4–5

THE REVELATION OF Jesus is the foundation of our Christianity, but we need to go deeper than that. Who do you *really* think Jesus is? This will determine how you relate to Him. Most Christians will say He is the Christ, the Son of God, but they do not really understand what that means. One of the most significant shifts in Scripture happens in Matthew 16:13–17:

> When Jesus came into the region of Caesarea Philippi, He asked His disciples, saying, "Who do men say that I, the Son of Man, am?" So they said, "Some say John the Baptist, some Elijah, and others Jeremiah or one of the prophets." He said to them, "But who do you say that I am?" Simon Peter answered and said, "You are the Christ, the Son of the living God." Jesus answered and said to him, "Blessed are you, Simon Bar-Jonah, for flesh and blood has not revealed this to you, but My Father who is in heaven."

The word *Christ* comes from the Greek word *Christos*, which means the Anointed One, Messiah, or Christ.[1] In the opening verse above, Simon Peter declared to Jesus that He was the One specifically anointed and appointed from God to bring salvation to the world.

Many see Jesus as a great teacher, an inspirational leader, and a religious figure. Even many Christians only see Jesus as an ever-loving, ever-forgiving, ever-accepting, gift-giving, non-judging, equity-restoring pacifist. Others see Jesus as an always-angry, constantly disappointed-in-them, distant God. How we see and perceive Jesus determines what we can receive from Him.

The revelation of Jesus releases the blessings of God upon your life. "Blessed are you, Simon Bar-Jonah" are the words Jesus spoke over Simon upon his declaration of the revelation of Jesus as the Christ.

So what was Jesus chosen and anointed to do? He gives us a very clear and specific answer in Luke 4:18–19: "The Spirit of the LORD is upon Me, because He has anointed Me to preach the gospel to the poor; He has sent Me to heal the brokenhearted, to proclaim liberty to the captives and recovery of sight to the blind, to set at liberty those who are oppressed; to proclaim the acceptable year of the LORD."

This passage tells us that God the Father anointed Christ to do six specific things:

1. Preach the gospel to the poor.

2. Heal the brokenhearted.

3. Proclaim liberty to the captives.

4. Recover sight to the blind.

5. Set at liberty those who are oppressed.

6. Proclaim the acceptable year of the Lord.

In today's study, we will examine each of these tasks in detail.

1. Preach the gospel to the poor. The word *poor* means "poor, destitute. *Refers to being poor, especially so poor as to be dependent on others for support.*"[2] Throughout human history the poor have been easy victims of the powerful. They rarely have opportunities to rise to a higher level, whether this is economically, politically, or societally. Jesus proclaimed that a new kingdom was coming. This kingdom of heaven would operate under the laws of heaven. Obedience to these kingdom laws would release the blessings of heaven.

The gospel of peace is the good news that humankind and

God would be one again. This gives hope to the hopeless. Christ declared that you can have an intimate personal relationship with God and walk in the divine favor of God regardless of your education, wealth, race, gender, age, or societal status. You do not have to earn this access to God's favor. You simply receive it by believing in Jesus and surrendering to His lordship.

This was a revolutionary concept when Jesus preached it. Before this, hopelessness reigned supreme. There were always the few rich and powerful, and then the masses of the poor and often oppressed. Only the special few had access to God, or "the gods," and to blessings and favor with men. Jesus was preaching a revolutionary concept—a new kingdom where the last would be first and the first would be last, a kingdom where God's favor is available to all who believe in Jesus.

Although some of the manifestations of the kingdom favor will be experienced here in this life, Jesus' focus was on the eternal kingdom. In that kingdom, "the last will be first, and the first last" (Matt. 20:16, MEV). The kingdom of heaven is where the smallest, weakest, and poorest on earth will be great, and they will sit on a throne. Christ preached of a future when He would rule and reign here on the earth with us. In this day all sin, wickedness, oppression, and death would be done away with.

From the beginning of His ministry Jesus the Christ was anointed to preach about a day when the words "Your kingdom come; Your will be done on earth, as it is in heaven" (Matt. 6:10, MEV) would be fulfilled. Jesus preached a message of hope for this life but even more so for the life to come.

To properly see Jesus as He is, you must understand the focus of His ministry. Jesus the Christ preached the gospel message with an eternal focus. If we only see Jesus as One who wants to bless us in this life and not One who works on an eternal plan for us, we will fail to understand much of what He does, how He does it, and why He does it.

2. Heal the brokenhearted. The second thing that Luke 4:18–19 says that Jesus the Christ will do is heal the brokenhearted. This word as used in the New Testament means to break in pieces, crush, or be battered.[3] The sense of the word is focused on your spirit. When your spirit is broken, crushed, and battered, it affects every part of your life.

"There is an enormous physical burden to being hurt and disappointed," says Karen Swartz, MD, director of the Mood Disorders Adult Consultation Clinic at Johns Hopkins Hospital.[4]

Scripture teaches us, "A merry heart does good like a medicine, but a broken spirit dries the bones" (Prov. 17:22, MEV), and, "The spirit of a man will sustain his infirmity, but a wounded spirit who can bear?" (Prov. 18:14, MEV).

Blood is created in the marrow of the bones. If the bones are dead and dry, no new blood is created. God says, "For the life of the flesh is in the blood" (Lev. 17:11, MEV). When we are wounded in our spirit, there is no flow of life. This leads to sickness, disease, and death. This is what happened in the Garden of Eden when man sinned against God. He was separated from the flow of the tree of life.

When man sinned, he was separated from God, and he became broken. His spirit was crushed in pieces, and a death process began in us. Jesus took on our brokenness and released spiritual healing in us.

> Surely He has borne our griefs and carried our sorrows; yet we esteemed Him stricken, smitten by God, and afflicted. But He was wounded for our transgressions, He was bruised [crushed] for our iniquities; the chastisement for our peace was upon Him, and by His stripes we are healed.
> —ISAIAH 53:4–5

Jesus the Christ came to release the words of healing that would produce life.

> He sent His word and healed them, and delivered them from their destructions.
> —PSALM 107:20

Jesus said, "The words that I speak to you are spirit and are life" (John 6:63, MEV). All the words of Jesus, when we believe them and obey, release healing to our broken hearts and produce life.

3. Proclaim liberty to the captives. The third truth stated in Luke 4:18–19 is that Jesus the Christ came to earth to proclaim liberty to the captives. Jesus quotes these verses from Isaiah 61. This, as with many Old Testament prophecies, has a dual fulfillment. The first was a declaration to the Jews during the Babylonian captivity. The second was the finished work of Christ on the cross. As King, Priest, and Prophet, Jesus was declaring that a final deliverance from sin, sickness, and death was coming.

Jesus pointed to the day when He would deliver us from living in a fallen world led by fallen men. It is significant that He quoted from Isaiah 61, because it promises a new kingdom here on earth during His millennial reign.

"So the Lord GOD will cause righteousness and praise to spring forth before all the nations" (Isa. 61:11, MEV). This verse also points to the promise of Isaiah 60:18: "Violence shall no more be heard in your land, nor devastation or destruction within your borders; but you shall call your walls Salvation and your gates Praise" (MEV).

The Christ was coming to deliver us from sin, sickness, and death and to establish His kingdom rule on the earth when He returns. The hope of salvation is the hope of the final salvation and deliverance from all the roots and consequences of sin.

4. Recover sight to the blind. Jesus was chosen and anointed to return sight to the blind as stated in the verses we read from Luke 4. This is not specifically mentioned in Isaiah 61, but it does appear in Isaiah 42:7: "To open blind eyes, to bring out the prisoners from the prison, and those who sit in darkness out of the prison house" (MEV).

Jesus the Christ came to give us "the Spirit of wisdom and revelation in the knowledge of Him" (Eph 1:17, MEV). As born-again believers, our spiritual eyes are somewhat open now, but there will come a day when we shall see all.

Now we see things imperfectly, like puzzling reflections
in a mirror, but then we will see everything with perfect
clarity. All that I know now is partial and incomplete, but
then I will know everything completely, just as God now
knows me completely.

—1 CORINTHIANS 13:12, NLT

Note that every one of these prophetic declarations about the
work of the Christ points to a partial but glorious experience
when we are born again, and then also a complete experience
when Jesus returns in the fullness of His glory.

Beloved, now we are children of God; and it has not yet
been revealed what we shall be, but we know that when
He is revealed, we shall be like Him, for we shall see Him
as He is. And everyone who has this hope in Him purifies
himself, just as He is pure.

—1 JOHN 3:2–3

5. Set at liberty those who are oppressed. The word *liberty*
means "pardon, forgiveness of sins."[5] The Christ came to break
the power of sin over us and to forgive our transgressions. The
phrase "set at liberty" in Luke 4:18 speaks of sending away and
forever pardoning our sins.

As far as the east is from the west, so far has He removed
our transgressions from us.

—PSALM 103:12

He will again have compassion on us, and will subdue
our iniquities. You will cast all our sins into the depths
of the sea.

—MICAH 7:19

When the Christ returns, He will subdue all nations and establish righteousness throughout the earth. The oppression caused by

our sins will be cast into the depths of the sea as far as the east is from the west.

6. Proclaim the acceptable year of the Lord. The sixth aspect of the Christ, the Messiah, as mentioned in the final sentence of Luke 4:18–19, is that He came to declare and bring about the day of God's favor, the season of grace. The word *acceptable* in relation to time is also used in the Old Testament when God speaks through the prophet Isaiah:

> Thus says the LORD: "In an acceptable time I have heard You, and in the day of salvation I have helped You; I will preserve You and give You as a covenant to the people, to restore the earth, to cause them to inherit the desolate heritages."
>
> —ISAIAH 49:8

The Christ has come to "restore the earth." Again, we see the dual focus of the salvation we receive upon our surrender to the lordship of Jesus and the future when we will rule and reign with Him here on the earth.

The acceptable year of the Lord speaks of God's grace. Grace is the favor of God that gives us access to the power of God for everything we need for life and godliness.

> Grace and peace be multiplied to you in the knowledge of God and of Jesus our Lord, as His divine power has given to us all things that pertain to life and godliness, through the knowledge of Him who called us by glory and virtue, by which have been given to us exceedingly great and precious promises, that through these you may be partakers of the divine nature, having escaped the corruption that is in the world through lust.
>
> —2 PETER 1:2–4

When you see the word *Christ*, meditate on His six purposes: 1) to preach the gospel to the poor; 2) to heal the brokenhearted; 3) to proclaim liberty to the captives; 4) to recover sight to the blind;

5) to set at liberty those who are oppressed; and 6) to proclaim the acceptable year of the Lord.

The Christ, the Anointed One, the Messiah, has come to bring the kingdom of heaven to the earth to be fully manifested when He returns. Let us see Jesus as He really is and understand that His mission was far greater than to forgive us of our sins. He came to restore all things; to deliver us from sin, sickness, and death; and to take full rulership of the earth.

Prayer

Father, in the name of Your Son Jesus, the Christ, I ask You to open my eyes to see Your eternal plan. Give me understanding into the depths of the revelation of the gospel. Heal me of my broken heart and release healing through me to a lost and dying world. Cause my heart and mind to dwell on the hope of the final salvation when Your Son Jesus returns to rule and reign on the earth. Grant unto me the Spirit of wisdom and revelation in the deep and intimate knowledge of You, and forgive me of all my sins as I forgive those who have sinned against me. Thank You that this is the day of salvation and the season of Your undeserved favor. Cause Your grace and favor to multiply in my life through a knowledge of You that never ends.

Day 5
THE FAITHFUL WITNESS

Grace to you and peace from Him who is and who was and who is to come...and from Jesus Christ, the faithful witness.
—REVELATION 1:4-5

JESUS IS DESCRIBED in Revelation chapter 1 as the faithful witness. This simple phrase is loaded with powerful revelation. When Jesus addressed the compromising church at Laodicea in Revelation 3:14, He declared that He was the faithful and true witness:

- Faithful: "trustworthy, pertaining to being reliable, implying worthy of full trust"[1]

- True: "real, not imaginary, being in accordance with fact"[2]

The Christians in Laodicea were comfortable in their prosperity and had compromised with the world, but Jesus reminded them that He alone was worthy of trust.

This message is for us as well. He is truth itself. Everything He says and does is real, not imaginary, and in accordance with fact.

Beholding Jesus as completely truthful and worthy of trust brings about a radical shift in how we perceive the circumstances of our lives. Many times, Christians question God. They look at the negative circumstances of their lives or the apparent blessings of those who do not serve God, and they question God's faithfulness.

Jesus is worthy of our complete and total trust. He has been faithful in all His Father's house and as a result is worthy of our complete trust. He was faithful unto death; therefore, you can trust Him completely with your life.

And all of us, as with unveiled face, [because we] continued to behold [in the Word of God] as in a mirror the
glory of the Lord, are constantly being transfigured into
His very own image in ever increasing splendor and from
one degree of glory to another; [for this comes] from the
Lord [Who is] the Spirit.

                                —2 CORINTHIANS 3:18, AMPC

In 1990 I had just gotten married, and we moved, by faith, to
Atlanta. I only had a small amount in savings, and I knew nobody
in the local area, but God had showed me in a vision a particular
church to attend. I somehow knew that I would become a staff
member at that church. At first I was so excited about this faith
journey that God sent us on. When the first month passed, however, I ran out of savings, but miraculously, enough money showed
up in the mail to pay the bills.

However, after two months, with no ministry job prospects, I
faced a large phone bill and had no way to pay it. I went to the
mailbox each day and laid hands on it and declared God's provision. Each day went by, and nothing was in the mail. The day
came when the phone company was going to shut off the line, and
I was going to be stuck in a strange city with no family or friends,
no job, and no money. The Lord had told me two years earlier that
I would never do secular work again.

I thought, "Well, maybe my wife can get a secular job while we
wait for this ministry job to manifest," but the Lord also told her
no.

I was faced with a desperate situation, but I went to the mailbox
as soon as the mail arrived. I was sure a big check would be in
there, but the box was empty.

Scared, dismayed, and confused, I went to the store and used
my last thirty-five cents to buy a newspaper. I brought it home and
turned to the classified ads. It was time to admit defeat and look
for a job. I said in my heart to God, "If You're not going to take
care of this family, I will."

My wife asked me what I was doing. I said, "I'm looking for a job." She sat there quietly, not saying anything. We both knew I was not supposed to do it. I went into my bedroom and prayed. I said to God, "I'm not accusing You of this, but it sure looks to me like You are reneging on Your covenant." Yes, I was questioning the faithfulness and truthfulness of God.

The Lord spoke something that pierced me through the heart. He said, "Son, will you trust Me even if they take the car, kick you out on the streets, and I lead you through total financial bankruptcy?"

This was not what I wanted to hear, but as the words came forth, God exposed my heart.

Was I willing to trust the faithfulness of God even if everything in my life collapsed? I responded immediately with repentance and said, "Yes, Lord, I will trust You no matter what happens."

Sure enough, the phone was shut off, and it was a day-to-day situation for a while, but God made a way. A few months later God supernaturally brought me to the church I had seen in the vision.

Beholding Jesus as completely faithful is a powerful weapon against the lies of the enemy. Eve believed the serpent's lies and questioned God's faithfulness and truthfulness. She rejected God's authority because she lost her trust in God.

This quality of Jesus' faithfulness and truthfulness is so profound that it is the name He is called when He returns on a white horse.

> Now I saw heaven opened, and behold, a white horse.
> And He who sat on him was called Faithful and True, and
> in righteousness He judges and makes war.
> —Revelation 19:11

The end times will be a season of intense upheavals, persecutions, deceptions, and confusion. The reality of what God does and allows to transpire through His judgment in removing everything that hinders love from the earth will shake much of our modern preaching and concepts of Jesus.

Jesus is worthy of your complete trust, even when everything has gone horribly wrong. When your prayers seem to be unanswered, when it appears that wickedness is winning, when tragedy strikes your household and the heavens feel like brass, Jesus remains faithful and true.

> God is not a man, that He should lie, nor a son of man,
> that He should repent. Has He said, and will He not do?
> Or has He spoken, and will He not make it good?
> —NUMBERS 23:19

It is utterly impossible for Jesus to be anything but faithful and true at all times. "If we are faithless, He remains faithful; He cannot deny Himself" (2 Tim. 2:13, MEV). The entirety of the universe is held together by the faithfulness and truth of His word. "He is the sole expression of the glory of God [the Light-being, the out-raying or radiance of the divine], and He is the perfect imprint and very image of [God's] nature, upholding and maintaining and guiding and propelling the universe by His mighty word of power" (Heb. 1:3, AMPC).

As Jesus declares, "Heaven and earth will pass away, but My words will never pass away" (Matt. 24:35, MEV).

If Jesus failed to be true and faithful for one moment, the entire universe would unravel. Jesus, the Word, upholds, maintains, guides, and propels the universe. God will not risk the loss of the entire universe just so He can be unfaithful to you. God's nature is faithfulness. He always is and always will be faithful.

When Moses asked to see God, he hid in the cleft of a rock. "Then the LORD descended in the cloud, and stood with him there, and proclaimed the name of the LORD. The LORD passed by before him, and proclaimed, 'The LORD, the LORD God, merciful and gracious, slow to anger, and abounding in goodness and truth'" (Exod. 34:5–6, MEV). The word *truth* here means "faithfulness, reliability, trustworthiness."[3]

When God declared His name and revealed His nature, He declared that He was faithful, reliable, and trustworthy. In doing so, God revealed to Moses that no matter what challenges we face, no matter what backslidings we are engaged in, no matter what armies rise up against us, God can be trusted to fulfill His promises.

This description of Jesus as the faithful witness reveals that He didn't come to testify of Himself, but rather to reveal the Father. "I have declared Your name to them, and will declare it, that the love with which You loved Me may be in them, and I in them" (John 17:26, MEV).

Jesus came to reveal who the Father is. He came to be a witness of what He has seen and heard from the Father. As we see Jesus, we also see the Father. Jesus declared, "He who has seen Me has seen the Father" (John 14:9, MEV), and, "If you had known Me, you would have known My Father also. From now on you do know Him and have seen Him" (John 14:7, MEV). Through Jesus we see who God the Father really is, for Jesus is the visible manifestation of the invisible God.

> He is the image of the invisible God, the firstborn over all creation. For by Him all things were created that are in heaven and that are on earth, visible and invisible, whether thrones or dominions or principalities or powers. All things were created through Him and for Him. And He is before all things, and in Him all things consist. And He is the head of the body, the church, who is the beginning, the firstborn from the dead, that in all things He may have the preeminence. For it pleased the Father that in Him all the fullness should dwell, and by Him to reconcile all things to Himself, by Him, whether things on earth or things in heaven, having made peace through the blood of His cross.
>
> —COLOSSIANS 1:15–20

Jesus is the faithful witness of all that God is and all that God has. Jesus came not to do His own will but the will of the One who sent Him. He said, "I have glorified You on the earth. I have finished the work You have given Me to do" (John 17:4, MEV).

We can place total and complete trust in Jesus because He fulfilled the will of His Father despite the incredible price He paid. He took on the form of man, died a sinner's death, rose from the dead, and is seated at the right hand of the throne of God. He is worthy of our complete trust.

Jesus earned the right of our complete trust because He was faithful to the Father. He was completely faithful to His Father to finish the work, and He will finish His work in you. "He who began a good work in you will perfect it until the day of Jesus Christ" (Phil. 1:6, MEV).

> Trust in the LORD, and do good; dwell in the land, and feed on His faithfulness. Delight yourself also in the LORD, and He shall give you the desires of your heart. Commit your way to the LORD, trust also in Him, and He shall bring it to pass.
>
> —PSALM 37:3–5

God promised that as we trust in Him and feed on His faithfulness, He will give us the desires of our hearts. He promised that as we commit our way to Him, He will bring it to pass, for He is faithful.

When we behold Jesus as the faithful witness, He imparts His faithfulness to us by His Holy Spirit. When we see Him as He is, we become like Him, and we also become faithful witnesses "[because we] continued to behold [in the Word of God] as in a mirror the glory of the Lord, are constantly being transfigured into His very own image in ever increasing splendor and from one degree of glory to another; [for this comes] from the Lord [Who is] the Spirit" (2 Cor. 3:18, AMPC).

Prayer

Father, I declare that Jesus is the faithful witness of all that You are and all that You possess. Reveal to me by Your Spirit the depth of this faithfulness, and fill my heart with absolute trust in You. I choose to believe that everything You speak will come to pass and that He who began a good work in me shall bring it to completion. I will trust in You, Lord, with all my heart and lean not unto my own understanding. In all my ways, let me see and know You. I repent of the times I have doubted You and trusted in another thought. Lord, I believe; help Thou my unbelief. Fill me with the power of the Holy Spirit to also be a faithful witness to all the world. May my life shine forth with Your glory that the world may see who You really are. In Jesus' name, amen.

Day 6
FIRSTBORN FROM THE DEAD

Grace to you and peace from Him who is and
who was and who is to come...and from Jesus
Christ...the firstborn from the dead.

—REVELATION 1:4–5

THE NEXT TWO descriptions in Revelation 1 are vitally connected. In both of these descriptions, the firstborn from the dead and the ruler of the kings of the earth, Jesus focuses us on our future eternal partnership with Him.

The revelation of Jesus as the firstborn from the dead is vital to our understanding of what God is doing in and through our lives. Something remarkable happened at the resurrection of Jesus. As important as the crucifixion was—Jesus died on the cross for our sins—the resurrection is more important. His death paid the price for our sins, but His resurrection gave us access to eternal life and our oneness with the Father.

Jesus was not the first person to be resurrected. Lazarus, the widow's son, and others were raised from the dead temporarily, but Jesus was the only One permanently raised from the dead—and He went further than that. He defeated death. He destroyed the power of death once and for all.

The focus of Jesus being the firstborn from the dead draws our hearts to several key realities.

Jesus is and remains fully human and fully divine. When Jesus was resurrected, He did not stop being human. He continued to have a human body, but it was fully God and supernatural. Jesus ate after He rose from the dead. He had Thomas put his finger into the holes in His hands and in His side as proof that He was crucified. He walked through a closed door in the Upper Room.

In the seventh chapter of his book, Daniel saw a *man* sitting on the throne of God:

> I was watching in the night visions, and behold, One like the Son of Man, coming with the clouds of heaven! He came to the Ancient of Days, and they brought Him near before Him. Then to Him was given dominion and glory and a kingdom, that all peoples, nations, and languages should serve Him. His dominion is an everlasting dominion, which shall not pass away, and His kingdom the one which shall not be destroyed.
>
> —Daniel 7:13–14

This prophetic vision was after Jesus' resurrection when He returned to heaven. When Jesus returns in His second coming, He will take full dominion over all the nations of the earth. Jesus, as a Man and as fully God, will physically rule and reign here on the earth.

Jesus conquered death so that whoever believes in Him will inherit everlasting life. The fact that Jesus rose from the dead and is alive gives us hope for the future, "knowing that He who raised the Lord Jesus will also raise us through Jesus" (2 Cor. 4:14, MEV).

The power of Jesus' resurrection can flow through our lives now and at the resurrection in fullness when we receive our heavenly bodies. "But if the Spirit of Him who raised Jesus from the dead lives in you, He who raised Christ from the dead will also give life to your mortal bodies through His Spirit that lives in you" (Rom. 8:11, MEV).

Firstborn **also points to Jesus' preeminence in all things.** He is and always will be first. He is above all and first and foremost of all. "He is the head of the body, the church. He is the beginning, the firstborn from the dead, so that in all things He may have the preeminence" (Col. 1:18, MEV).

In the focus of prophetic Scripture we see the importance of this truth in regard to the end times. Psalm 2 is an end-time prophetic psalm that is broken down into three main areas. The first area is the wickedness of man to attempt to thwart the influence and authority of God on the earth.

> Why do the nations rage, and the people plot a vain thing? The kings of the earth set themselves, and the rulers take counsel together, against the LORD and against His Anointed, saying, "Let us break Their bonds in pieces and cast away Their cords from us."
> —PSALM 2:1–3

First it speaks of a day when the world rulers will plot together to cast aside God's Word, His holiness, and His rightful claim over the affairs of man. We already see this happening today in the LGBTQ agenda, in humanistic philosophies, and in the redefining of what constitutes love. We see this in the effort to push the Bible and prayer out of public life, and to criminalize the preaching of holiness and repentance. The rulers of this world are plotting together to destroy the power and influence of God and His church.

Unfortunately this is also happening within the church under the guise of being free from legalism and a religious spirit. Just like the world leaders, many emerging church leaders have cast off the "restraints" of God's Word about holy living. They "come and stand before Me in this house, which is called by My name, and say, 'We are delivered,' so that you may do all these abominations" (Jer. 7:10, MEV).

The second part of Psalm 2 is the Father's response:

> He who sits in the heavens shall laugh; the LORD shall hold them in derision. Then He shall speak to them in His wrath, and distress them in His deep displeasure: "Yet I have set My King on My holy hill of Zion."
> —PSALM 2:4–6

The Father declares that no matter what they plan, He has already set in motion His plan to set His King above all the nations of the earth. God gave man authority and dominion on the earth.

The gifts and call of God are without repentance. Therefore, it must be a man, His Begotten, who is fully God and fully man, who will be the One who sits on the throne over the kingdoms of this world. This man (Jesus) whom the Father has chosen will rule from Jerusalem.

The third section is Jesus' response to the Father:

> I will declare the decree: The LORD has said to Me, "You are My Son, today I have begotten You. Ask of Me, and I will give You the nations for Your inheritance, and the ends of the earth for Your possession. You shall break them with a rod of iron; you shall dash them to pieces like a potter's vessel."
>
> —PSALM 2:7–9

Jesus says the Father speaks to Him and says, "Today I have begotten You." There is debate as to when this took place. Some believe God "begot" Jesus through the immaculate conception. Truly the Father does declare of Jesus while He is walking the earth, "This is My beloved Son, in whom I am well pleased" (Matt. 3:17, MEV). However, in Acts 13:33–34, Luke ties together Psalm 2 and the resurrection as pointing to the same event: "God has fulfilled this for us their children, in that He has raised up Jesus. As it is also written in the second Psalm: 'You are My Son, today I have begotten You.' And that He raised Him from the dead, no more to return to corruption, He has spoken thus." At the resurrection, Jesus shed the limitations of the temporal human body and became a new creation, wholly man and wholly God. He took on a perfect eternal body.

In the resurrected body of Jesus, He displays the glory of this new creation. "Beloved, now we are children of God; and it has not yet been revealed what we shall be, but we know that when He is revealed, we shall be like Him, for we shall see Him as He is. And everyone who has this hope in Him purifies himself, just as He is pure" (1 John 3:2–3).

Jesus being the firstborn of us all is the guarantee of what we

are becoming. "For those whom He foreknew, He predestined to
be conformed to the image of His Son, so that He might be the
firstborn among many brothers" (Rom. 8:29, MEV).

The power of the resurrection is the hope of our future, and it
delivers us from the fear of death in this life. This power is displayed through the Spirit of holiness. When we see Jesus as the
firstborn from the dead, we also see the fullness of His holiness.
The public declaration of Jesus' preeminence and the rightful heir
of all things as the Father's firstborn Son is displayed through the
power of the Spirit of holiness when Jesus was raised from the
dead. Only One was worthy to escape and conquer the death that
came into the world through original sin.

> Concerning His Son Jesus Christ our Lord, who was born
> of the seed of David according to the flesh, and declared
> to be the Son of God with power according to the Spirit
> of holiness, by the resurrection from the dead. Through
> Him we have received grace and apostleship for obedi-
> ence to the faith among all nations for His name, among
> whom you also are the called of Jesus Christ.
>
> —ROMANS 1:3–6

> For if we have been united together in the likeness of His
> death, certainly we also shall be in the likeness of His res-
> urrection, knowing this, that our old man was crucified
> with Him, that the body of sin might be done away with,
> that we should no longer be slaves of sin. For he who has
> died has been freed from sin. Now if we died with Christ,
> we believe that we shall also live with Him, knowing that
> Christ, having been raised from the dead, dies no more.
> Death no longer has dominion over Him. For the death
> that He died, He died to sin once for all; but the life that
> He lives, He lives to God. Likewise you also, reckon your-
> selves to be dead indeed to sin, but alive to God in Christ
> Jesus our Lord.
>
> —ROMANS 6:5–11

The power of the Spirit of holiness was demonstrated through Jesus' resurrection and will be displayed again through our resurrection. This is one of the reasons why the removal of a focus on holiness in much of today's teachings is so far from the gospel. The working of the Spirit of holiness and Jesus' resurrection are intricately tied together and will be forever. Only through holiness will we see Jesus as He is, the firstborn from the dead. "Pursue peace with all men, and holiness without which no one will see the Lord" (Heb. 12:14, MEV).

As we go through the struggles and battles of this life, we have an eternal hope. This hope does not disappoint. We look unto Jesus as the firstborn from the dead to see who we shall be.

> So also is the resurrection of the dead. The body is sown in corruption, it is raised in incorruption. It is sown in dishonor, it is raised in glory. It is sown in weakness, it is raised in power. It is sown a natural body, it is raised a spiritual body. There is a natural body, and there is a spiritual body. And so it is written, "*The first man Adam became a living being.*" The last Adam became a life-giving spirit.
> —1 CORINTHIANS 15:42–45, EMPHASIS ADDED

Glory be to God. We shall also bear the image of Christ for eternity. We shall have the same heavenly body. Only our new heavenly body can fully inherit the kingdom of God. Jesus came not only declaring a way for our sins to be forgiven, but that through His resurrection we will enter a new kingdom and a new realm of existence. We shall become like Him.

> Now this I say, brethren, that flesh and blood cannot inherit the kingdom of God; nor does corruption inherit incorruption. Behold, I tell you a mystery: We shall not all sleep, but we shall all be changed—in a moment, in the twinkling of an eye, at the last trumpet. For the trumpet will sound, and the dead will be raised incorruptible, and we shall be changed. For this corruptible must put on

incorruption, and this mortal must put on immortality.
So when this corruptible has put on incorruption, and
this mortal has put on immortality, then shall be brought
to pass the saying that is written: *"Death is swallowed up
in victory. O Death, where is your sting? O Hades, where
is your victory?"*
—1 CORINTHIANS 15:50–55, EMPHASIS ADDED

Even Paul at the end of his life was consumed with this concept
of the resurrected Christ. He longed to be conformed into this
existence and wanted to fully behold and experience it.

> That I may know Him and the power of His resurrection,
> and the fellowship of His sufferings, being conformed to
> His death, if, by any means, I may attain to the resurrec-
> tion from the dead.
—PHILIPPIANS 3:10–11

Today there is almost no teaching on the resurrection from the
dead and our future life. However, in the early church it was one
of the six foundational doctrines of Christ.

> Therefore, leaving the discussion of the elementary prin-
> ciples of Christ, let us go on to perfection, not laying
> again the foundation of repentance from dead works
> and of faith toward God, of the doctrine of baptisms, of
> laying on of hands, of resurrection of the dead, and of
> eternal judgment. And this we will do if God permits.
—HEBREWS 6:1–3

This focus on the future kingdom and future hope gave the
saints amazing power to stand in the face of deadly hostility.
Meditate on this reality that you are going to have a new eternal
spiritual body like Jesus. Ask the Holy Spirit to reveal to you Jesus
as the firstborn from the dead.

> Blessed be the God and Father of our Lord Jesus Christ,
> who according to His abundant mercy has begotten us

again to a living hope through the resurrection of Jesus Christ from the dead, to an inheritance incorruptible and undefiled and that does not fade away, reserved in heaven for you, who are kept by the power of God through faith for salvation ready to be revealed in the last time.

—1 Peter 1:3–5

Prayer

Father, in the name of Your Son Jesus, fill me with wisdom and revelation on the power of the resurrection. Let me see Jesus as first in all things. Let me begin to glimpse the glory of this new reality of Jesus as fully man and fully God for all eternity. Let me know this hope of His calling so I can become a body wholly filled and flooded with You. Cause all fear of death and suffering in this life to flee from me as I am filled with this hope of eternal life.

I choose this day to stop focusing so much of my attention on the affairs of this life and to begin to focus on the eternal resurrected life with You. Fill my heart with this hope that causes me to purify myself. Like Paul, I pray that I may know Jesus and the power of His resurrection (Phil. 3:10). In Jesus' holy name, amen.

Day 7
RULER OVER THE KINGS OF THE EARTH

Grace to you and peace from Him who is and
who was and who is to come...and from Jesus
Christ...the ruler over the kings of the earth.
—REVELATION 1:4–5

IN REVELATION 1 we see a consistent theme in the descriptions of Jesus. There is a focus on the power, authority, and rulership of Jesus now and in the age to come. In this daily devotional, there are two areas we need to focus on. First is the rulership that Jesus exercises now over the kings of the earth, and second is the future rulership that will come when He returns. They are not the same.

The confusion over this distinction causes many Christians to relate incorrectly to governing authorities.

> And He changes the times and the seasons; He removes kings and raises up kings; He gives wisdom to the wise and knowledge to those who have understanding. He reveals deep and secret things; He knows what is in the darkness, and light dwells with Him.
> —DANIEL 2:21–22

Daniel was about to reveal the interpretation of the dream Nebuchadnezzar had received. The dream was about the coming of successive kingdoms: their rise and fall, and ultimately the rise and eternal rule of the kingdom of heaven on the earth.

> And in the days of these kings the God of heaven will set up a kingdom which shall never be destroyed; and the kingdom shall not be left to other people; it shall break

in pieces and consume all these kingdoms, and it shall
stand forever.

—DANIEL 2:44

It is very important that we understand that simply because
God raised up a kingdom does not mean we must submit to those
kings' (authorities') demands. In recent years we saw this con-
flict play out around the world with COVID-19 and the closing of
churches worldwide.

A great debate raged within the body of Christ as to the correct response to the churches being ordered to close. Many quoted
Romans 13:1–2: "Let every person be subject to the governing
authorities, for there is no authority except from God, and those
that exist are appointed by God. Therefore whoever resists the
authority resists what God has appointed, and those who resist
will incur judgment" (MEV).

A large majority of pastors and Christians pointed to these
verses and said we *must* obey the government and close our doors
because God says He appointed them. The problem is in con-
flating the truth that all authority comes from God and submit-
ting to ungodly commands.

Let us again look at the story of Daniel. Daniel made some very
powerful declarations about Nebuchadnezzar. He said, "For the
God of heaven has given you a kingdom, power, strength, and
glory....He has given them into your hand and has made you ruler
over them all" (Dan. 2:37–38, MEV).

Daniel recognized God's authority given to the king. So, under
modern interpretation, Daniel should have submitted to the king's
decrees. We know that Daniel and the Hebrew children repeatedly
did not submit to the kings. They did not bow and worship the
false idol. They did not stop their time of committed prayer. Yes,
in Daniel's day, Darius the king ordered everyone to *stop* praying
to anyone but him. In modern terms King Darius ordered them
to yield to his wisdom and decrees and not to God's commands.

Daniel was one of three governors and was considered by the
king to be the highest authority in the land, except the king of

course. One of the men approached the king and said, "Have you not signed a decree, that every man who asks a petition of any god or man within thirty days, save of you, O king, shall be cast into the den of lions?" Then the king answered, "The thing is true, according to the law of the Medes and Persians, which may not be altered" (Dan. 6:12, MEV).

Evil men within the government of Darius feared and hated Daniel's wisdom, power, and influence. So they plotted to destroy Daniel. He was a faithful man, which meant they could not destroy him by his character, so they came up with a trap. They said to themselves, "We shall not find any charge against this Daniel unless we find it against him concerning the law of his God" (Dan. 6:5).

I want you to note this. They wanted to set Daniel up to have to choose between obeying God or the king. They knew that if he disobeyed God, he would lose favor with God and thus no longer be a threat, but if he obeyed God and disobeyed the king, he would lose favor with the king and be killed. Either way, Daniel was trapped.

> So these governors and satraps thronged before the king, and said thus to him: "King Darius, live forever! All the governors of the kingdom, the administrators and satraps, the counselors and advisors, have consulted together to establish a royal statute and to make a firm decree, that whoever petitions any god or man for thirty days, except you, O king, shall be cast into the den of lions."
> —DANIEL 6:6–7

There was a consensus among all the leaders that for the next thirty days they must come to the king and only the king for any petitions, needs, or requests. Sound familiar?

Daniel did not obey man. He obeyed God and was thrown into the lion's den. The lion's den was a place of sure destruction. If you obeyed God and not the king, the king would cause you to be devoured. It's as if they were saying, "If you dare meet in church gatherings, we will fine you, arrest you, take your church from you. We will throw you into the lion's den." During the pandemic lockdown of 2020–2021, many pastors yielded to the decrees of men and not the command of God: "Let us not forsake the assembling of ourselves together, as is the manner of some, but let us exhort one another, especially as you see the Day approaching" (Heb. 10:25, MEV).

We found a multitude of excuses and surrendered our platforms to ungodly organizations like Facebook and YouTube. We replaced in-person fellowship and corporate worship with posting comments while sipping our coffee in our PJs. We replaced visiting the sick with social distancing. We replaced laying down our lives with running for our lives. We bowed our knee and obeyed the unrighteous decree. Many did this because they did not understand what is meant when we call Jesus the ruler of the kings of the earth.

The Book of Revelation is about Jesus, who is coming back to rule and reign here on the earth as righteous judge. The entire focus of Jesus is the end of the age when He will judge the wicked, remove everything that is contrary to His righteousness, and rule and reign over the nations of the earth.

The description of Jesus as the ruler of the kings of the earth is to cause us to focus on the future hope that we have when Jesus will do whatever it takes to remove all wickedness and bring about His kingdom here on the earth. When we see all the wickedness that is and will increase in the world, we need to keep our eyes on this hope. Jesus is not going to come in the sky, take us away with Him into heaven, and destroy the earth while we sit around the throne playing harps and singing all day.

No, my dear friends, Jesus is coming back to take over this earth and to rule and reign with us for a thousand years. Jesus, at the appointed time, will come and deliver His bride from a wicked and cruel world. He will establish true righteousness and justice in all nations. Jesus will lead all the nations as the King of kings.

> Oh, let the nations be glad and sing for joy! For You shall judge the people righteously, and govern the nations on earth. Selah
>
> —PSALM 67:4

Say among the nations, "The LORD reigns; the world also
is firmly established, it shall not be moved; He shall judge
the peoples righteously." Let the heavens rejoice, and let
the earth be glad; let the sea roar, and all its fullness; let
the field be joyful, and all that is in it. Then all the trees of
the woods will rejoice before the LORD. For He is coming,
for He is coming to judge the earth. He shall judge the
world with righteousness, and the peoples with His truth.

—PSALM 96:10–13

Now I saw heaven opened, and behold, a white horse.
And He who sat on him was called Faithful and True,
and in righteousness He judges and makes war. His eyes
were like a flame of fire, and on His head were many
crowns. He had a name written that no one knew except
Himself. He was clothed with a robe dipped in blood, and
His name is called The Word of God. And the armies in
heaven, clothed in fine linen, white and clean, followed
Him on white horses. Now out of His mouth goes a sharp
sword, that with it He should strike the nations. And He
Himself will rule them with a rod of iron. He Himself
treads the winepress of the fierceness and wrath of
Almighty God. And He has on His robe and on His thigh
a name written: KING OF KINGS AND LORD OF LORDS.

—REVELATION 19:11–16

As we begin to see Jesus as the ruler of the kings of the earth, a
new rejoicing and prophetic praise will rise up in our hearts.

Shout joyfully to the LORD, all the earth; break forth in
song, rejoice, and sing praises. Sing to the LORD with the
harp, with the harp and the sound of a psalm, with trumpets and the sound of a horn; shout joyfully before the
LORD, the King....For He is coming to judge the earth.
With righteousness He shall judge the world, and the
peoples with equity.

—PSALM 98:4–9

When the world turns from God, sin abounds, and injustice seems to be everywhere, we must remember a day is coming when all will be defeated. Yes, today we can begin to exercise this righteous rulership of Jesus in every sphere of society, but the fullness will happen when He returns.

As long as the devil and his demons are allowed to operate, we will not see the fullness of Jesus' rulership in the earth. Yes, Jesus is presently the ruler of the kings of the earth, but in His mercy and long-suffering He allows some wickedness to continue. Jesus has the devil on a leash and uses him for His eternal purposes.

Jesus taught in the parable of the tares and wheat about the sons of the devil and the sons of righteousness existing together. He said, "Let both grow together until the harvest," and then, "Therefore as the weeds are gathered and burned in the fire, so shall it be in the end of this world" (Matt. 13:30, 40, MEV). He does this for several reasons.

- He gives people time to repent: when speaking to the church at Thyatira, whose prophetess Jezebel was falsely teaching that Christians were free to engage in sexual immorality and idol worship, Jesus said, "I gave her time to repent of her sexual immorality, and she did not repent" (Rev. 2:21, MEV).

- He allows their guilt to rise to its fullness to establish that He is ultimately just to judge them: "For you, brethren, became imitators of the churches of God which are in Judea in Christ Jesus. For you also suffered the same things from your own countrymen, just as they did from the Judeans, who killed both the Lord Jesus and their own prophets, and have persecuted us; and they do not please God and are contrary to all men, forbidding us to speak to the Gentiles that they may be saved, so as always to fill up the measure of their sins; but

wrath has come upon them to the uttermost"
(1 Thess. 2:14–16).

- To test His people: "My brethren, count it all joy
  when you fall into various trials, knowing that
  the testing of your faith produces patience. But let
  patience have its perfect work, that you may be perfect and complete, lacking nothing" (Jas. 1:2–4).

Jesus is in total control, even when it seems like wickedness and
darkness is winning. The absolute authority of Jesus is immutable.
It can never be removed or replaced. It lasts forever.

But now we see times when it does not look like that. What is
our role now, in partnership with Jesus, in exercising His kingdom
authority on the earth before His return? It is clear from Scripture
that Christianity will not take full and complete authority over
wickedness and darkness until Jesus' return. Are we just to sit
back, tuck our heads in the sand, and wait for the rapture? God
forbid. We, as joint heirs with Christ, have been commissioned to
release His kingdom authority into the earth.

We exercise His authority in the earth now through the gospel.
Let us focus for a moment on a few ways we release Jesus' kingdom
authority into the earth before His return.

- We preach the gospel of the kingdom.

  > And this gospel of the kingdom will be
  > preached in all the world as a witness to all
  > the nations, and then the end will come.
  > —MATTHEW 24:14

  > Go into all the world and preach the gospel
  > to every creature. He who believes and is
  > baptized will be saved; but he who does not
  > believe will be condemned.
  > —MARK 16:15–16

- We declare through prophetic prayer and worship
  that the legal authority of heaven will be done in
  the earth.

> I will give you the keys of the kingdom of
> heaven; and whatever you bind (declare to
> be improper and unlawful) on earth must be
> what is already bound in heaven; and what-
> ever you loose (declare lawful) on earth must
> be what is already loosed in heaven.
> —MATTHEW 16:19, AMPC

> In this manner, therefore, pray: Our Father
> in heaven, hallowed be Your name. Your
> kingdom come. Your will be done.
> —MATTHEW 6:9–10

- We are to influence every area of society by being
  engaged in all areas of influence while living our
  lives in submission to Jesus' authority. Some call it
  the seven mountains of influence: religion, family,
  education, government, media, arts and entertainment, and business. Jesus gave us this command in
  the Sermon on the Mount.

> You are the salt of the earth; but if the salt
> loses its flavor, how shall it be seasoned? It is
> then good for nothing but to be thrown out
> and trampled underfoot by men. You are the
> light of the world. A city that is set on a hill
> cannot be hidden. Nor do they light a lamp
> and put it under a basket, but on a lampstand,
> and it gives light to all who are in the house.
> Let your light so shine before men, that they
> may see your good works and glorify your
> Father in heaven.
> —MATTHEW 5:13–16

We are not to hide in our little Christian communities and wait for Jesus to come back. We are to be bold proclaimers of Jesus' legal authority as ruler of the kings of the earth. We are to preach, pray, and live in submission to, in partnership with, and as examples of Jesus' legal authority over all.

> Therefore God also has highly exalted Him and given Him the name which is above every name, that at the name of Jesus every knee should bow, of those in heaven, and of those on earth, and of those under the earth, and that every tongue should confess that Jesus Christ is Lord, to the glory of God the Father.
>
> —PHILIPPIANS 2:9–11

As we go through this life and see the injustices around us, let us stand strong, bold, and confident because we know that Jesus is the ruler of the kings of the earth.

Prayer

Father, open our eyes to see Jesus as the righteous king and ruler of all the nations and authorities. Help us place our hope in You that Jesus will soon return and defeat everything that hinders Your kingdom and love from being fully experienced and manifested in the earth. Give us understanding as to how to walk in kingdom authority now while You are placing everything under Jesus' feet. Fill our hearts with joy and rejoicing as we know that You are in ultimate control and no weapon formed against You or Your church shall prosper. We thank You that You are the righteous judge and King, and that the whole earth is going to be filled with Your glory. In Jesus' name, amen.

Day 8
JESUS WHO LOVED US

Grace to you and peace from Him who is and who was and who is to come...and from Jesus Christ...who loved us and washed us from our sins in His own blood.

—REVELATION 1:4–5

THE UNVEILING OF Jesus as the Christ, the faithful witness, the firstborn from the dead, and the ruler of the kings of the earth has shown us who Jesus is and what He is focused on. Now Jesus unveils to us the divine motivation behind His actions. He wants us to focus on the driving force behind all that He has done for us and why He will do all the things He revealed about the end times. However, unless we grasp His divine motivation and ultimate plan, many will be overcome by the intensity of the days ahead.

Whether you believe you are here during the tribulation period or not, the events of the world are accelerating and rapidly becoming more extreme. When we have a better understanding of Jesus—why He died for us and what He will do in the future—we will have a firm foundation in days of trouble, now and in the future.

Why did God create mankind? What was His divine purpose and intention? Why did Jesus have to come to earth as a man? Why did He have to shed His blood? What was it about mankind that motivated God to deal with us differently than with the rest of His creation?

> What is man that You are mindful of him, or the son of man that You take care of him? You have made him a little lower than the angels; You have crowned him with glory and honor, and set him over the works of Your hands. You have put all things in subjection under his feet.
>
> —HEBREWS 2:6–8

In my book *Satan's Big Fat Lie*, I deal extensively with the concept of God's purpose for creating us.

> The real power of the revelation of God's love comes
> when we see the motive of God's love. As long as we
> see God's fiery desire for us through the lens of how it
> benefits us, we are prone to the lies of shame that cause
> us to withdraw from God. We start hearing lies in our
> head such as, "How can God love me? Look how much I
> messed up. I'm not worthy; I'm not good enough; I'm not
> strong enough."[1]

When we focus on ourselves, whether positively or negatively, we tend to fall into Satan's traps. We must look unto Jesus. God loves us because of and for His good pleasure, will, plan, and eternal purpose, not because of how good or worthy we are. Only Jesus is worthy.

John 3:35 tells us, "The Father loves the Son, and has given all things into His hand." The Father gave us to Jesus because He loved Jesus and foreordained us to be the bride of Christ. Jesus loves the Father and will do the will of the Father above all things to bring Him pleasure. Jesus loves us with the same love with which He loves the Father because the Father chose us in Him before the foundation of the world to be the bride of Christ. Five times in Jesus' final prayer in John 17 He says that the Father gave us to Him. We are a gift from the Father to Jesus.

Let me put it this way. Jesus' love for you is so intense because you were specifically chosen by His Father to be His precious, eternal bride. You are God's best and perfect eternal gift to His Son. You and I are the ones God Himself chose to share all of Himself with and to dwell in for all eternity. "And you are in Him, made full and having come to fullness of life [in Christ you too are filled with the Godhead—Father, Son and Holy Spirit—and reach full spiritual stature]" (Col. 2:10, AMPC).

Paul unveils the mystery of the gospel when he writes, "'For this reason a man shall leave his father and mother and shall be joined to his wife, and the two shall be one flesh.' This is a great mystery, but I am speaking about Christ and the church" (Eph. 5:31–32, MEV). Paul is pointing to the deep truth that Christ and the church shall be joined in the same way that a man and a woman are joined in marriage. The two shall become one flesh.

Jesus' desire and love for us is not just as mere humans or just another of His creations. We were created to be His eternal bride. God created us to be just like Him so that we could fully engage in this divine eternal union: "That they may all be one, as You, Father, are in Me, and I in You. May they also be one in Us, that the world may believe that You have sent Me" (John 17:21, MEV).

When we sinned, it separated us from the life of God. When "God formed man from the dust of the ground and breathed into his nostrils the breath of life...man became a living being" (Gen. 2:7, MEV). God gave man access to eternal life as manifested in the tree of life, but God gave man a grave warning: "Of the tree of the knowledge of good and evil you shall not eat, for in the day that you eat from it you will surely die" (Gen. 2:17, MEV).

Man ate of that tree, and this act of disobedience caused man to be separated from the divine life of God. Immediately upon man's disobedience, the death process began, and the divine judgment of God was required, for God is eternally just. Death, sin, and rebellion are like leavening that spoils the whole batch. It spreads and destroys, and therefore it must be eradicated. Sin separates us from the life flow of God.

God's holiness will literally consume anything that is not in perfect union with Him. When Moses asked to see God's glory, the fullness of who God really was, God said it was impossible in man's fallen state.

"Then Moses said, 'I pray, show me Your glory.' Then He said, 'I will make all My goodness pass before you, and I will proclaim the name of the LORD before you.'...He said, 'You cannot see My face, for no man shall see Me and live'" (Exod. 33:18–20, MEV).

This separation of man in his sinful state would make the eternal marriage of the Lamb to His bride impossible. Jesus loved the Father, and Jesus loved the Father's gift, His bride. Jesus' perfect love for us was driven by far more than who we are, but that we were specifically created by His Father, unique above all creation, to be able to fully share and participate in an eternal love relationship with the fullness of all that God is and all that God has: His glory.

By the time Moses said this to God, man had been sinful for many generations since the Garden of Eden. His bloodline was permanently affected. Instead of the breath of God—His divine eternal life from generation to generation—death had passed from generation to generation forever. "Therefore as sin came into the world through one man and death through sin, so death has spread to all men, because all have sinned" (Rom. 5:12, MEV). "For just as through one man's disobedience the many were made sinners" (Rom. 5:19, MEV).

One man, Adam, released death instead of life into all humanity. A great mystery was revealed in this unique verse as God was giving the law. The law was given to reveal God's holiness and nature, but the law did not have the power to deliver us from the work of death in our bodies. It could only expose that we had this sin nature in us.

God reveals that this divine life was to be carried through a specific part of our bodies. This is the part that He originally breathed the breath of life into. When God breathed into man, His divine life entered the lungs of the newly created man and into the blood. When God breathed into Adam's lungs, His divine life transferred into Adam's blood. This is why God said in Leviticus 17:11, "For the life of the flesh is in the blood, and I have given it to you on the altar to make atonement for your lives; for it is the blood that makes atonement for the soul" (MEV).

When He said this, God pointed us to the source of man's problem, but He also revealed the solution. When we sinned, we lost our connection to the eternal divine life of God. Just like all aspects of creation, we were now subject to decay, sickness, disease, and death. God started to reveal through the law about blood and especially through the sacrifices that the key to reconciling this eternal separation from God's original plan was to be found in the blood.

Of course, "it is not possible that the blood of bulls and goats could take away sins" (Heb. 10:4). However, God was pointing us to our eternal problem and His eternal solution. The Father turned to His Son and said, "I need You to leave the glory that You have with Me and go and rescue Your bride." The only way for justice to be fulfilled was for a man to die.

"For the wages of sin is death" (Rom. 6:23). "There is none righteous, no, not one" (Rom. 3:10). "For all have sinned and fall short of the glory of God" (Rom. 3:23).

Man sinned; therefore, a man must die. The death cycle must be broken.

Because a man sinned, only a *man* could pay the price. Either the Father had to immediately judge and permanently remove Adam and thus all mankind from His eternal presence, or He had to have another who would take Adam's place and pay the price for Adam's guilt. The problem is that only a man who still had the divine life perfectly flowing through Him could qualify to be a worthy substitute.

Man sinned, so it had to be a man, but a man without sin, a man still filled with the divine life of God. However, Scripture declares, "Through one man sin entered the world, and death through sin, and thus death spread to all men" (Rom. 5:12), and, "There is none righteous, no, not one...for all have sinned and fall short of the glory of God" (Rom. 3:10, 23).

An eternal problem existed; man was incapable of redeeming himself. He could not be his own sacrifice and fulfill God's eternal love story to be the bride of Christ. This was the problem, but God had a solution: "For what the law could not do...God did by sending His own Son in the likeness of sinful flesh, and concerning sin, He condemned sin in the flesh" (Rom. 8:3, MEV).

Jesus had to leave the glory of heaven and become fully man. Jesus "emptied Himself, taking upon Himself the form of a servant, and was made in the likeness of men. And being found in the form of a man, He humbled Himself and became obedient to death, even death on a cross" (Phil. 2:7–8, MEV).

Only One could save us who "was in every sense tempted like

we are, yet without sin" (Heb. 4:15, MEV). Only a man who was filled with the divine eternal life of God and lived a sinless human life could be an adequate substitute for us and take our guilt to the cross.

The Father "made Him who knew no sin to be sin for us, that we might become the righteousness of God in Him" (2 Cor. 5:21, MEV). This includes all our guilt, all our sin, and all our rebellion. As Isaiah 53:6 tells us, "the LORD has laid on Him the iniquity of us all" (MEV). The sin of every murderer, rapist, liar, thief, adulterer, abuser, sexually immoral person, those who are prideful and unforgiving, and sorcerers and those engaged in witchcraft all filled Jesus' body while He was on the cross. Jesus literally became sin. He was so filled with our sins that the Father turned His face from Jesus and could no longer look upon Him. This is why "Jesus cried out with a loud voice, saying, *'Eloi, Eloi, lama sabachthani?'* which means, 'My God, My God, why have You forsaken Me?'" (Mark 15:34, MEV).

Some may say the Father did not turn His face from Jesus, but remember what God told Moses: "You cannot see My face; for no man [sinful man] shall see Me, and live" (Exod. 33:20). Jesus was beaten, tortured, scorned, and crucified on a cross, and then He died on that cross because of His love for us. Only God could take the form of a man and substitute Himself for the guilty. He didn't have to. The Father could have removed us from His presence to spend eternity in the lake of fire, and then started over. But "He chose us in Him before the foundation of the world, that we should be holy and without blame before Him in love" (Eph. 1:4).

> He is so rich in kindness and grace that he purchased our freedom with the blood of his Son and forgave our sins. He has showered his kindness on us, along with all wisdom and understanding. God has now revealed to us his mysterious will regarding Christ—*which is to fulfill his own good plan.*
>
> —Ephesians 1:7–9, NLT, emphasis added

Jesus' love for us is unshakable, unending, and unlimited because we are the best gift the Father gave to the Son. Meditate on it like this: You may have a precious piece of jewelry. It is your favorite and most valuable. If you lose it, your heart may be sad, but usually you can replace it with another one. However, if it was your mother's and she gave it to you as a gift, if you lose it, it becomes irreplaceable. It's irreplaceable because you can always create another piece of jewelry, but you can't replace the fact that it was a gift given in love.

Likewise, God the Father gave you and me as a gift to Jesus. The Father could have destroyed mankind and started again, but that still wouldn't change the fact that we were created as His gift to Jesus as an eternal bride.

In John 17, Jesus says in His prayer to the Father, "They were Yours, You gave them to Me, and they have kept Your word....I pray for them...whom You have given Me, for they are Yours.... Father, I desire that they also whom You gave Me may be with Me where I am" (vv. 6, 9, 24).

Before we end this day, let us focus on Revelation 1:5: "To Him who loved us and washed us from our sins in His own blood."

Prayer

Thank You, Father, for Your eternal plan and wisdom. Thank You that You created me to be the bride of Christ. You created me so that You could share all that You are and all that You possess for all eternity. You planned for me to experience the fullness of Your love and become a body wholly filled with You. Thank You for Your love for me manifested by sending Jesus in a weak, human vessel to walk a sinless life and sacrifice Himself for my sin and rebellion. Thank You for the blood that Christ shed for me. I place all my trust in the totality of the price paid. I do not trust in my own good works but in the shed blood of Jesus. Thank You that Jesus didn't stay in the grave, but He was raised from the dead and conquered death forever. Thank You, Father, thank You, my beloved Jesus, for Your love and Your blood. Help me to experience the fullness of Your love and the power of Your blood. In Jesus' name, amen.

Day 9
WE ARE A KINGDOM OF PRIESTS

[He] made us kings and priests to His God and Father.
—REVELATION 1:6

J ESUS LOVED US and washed us so we could be His bride and
function as a kingdom of priests unto His Father.

The phrase "kings and priests" is probably better translated as
"a kingdom of priests," according to the *Commentary Critical and
Explanatory on the Whole Bible*. They shall share His King-Priest
throne in the millennial kingdom.[1]

God has always established that He wanted a priesthood to
minister to Him and for Him.

> Now therefore, if you will indeed obey My voice and keep
> My covenant, then you shall be a special treasure to Me
> above all people; for all the earth is Mine. And you shall
> be to Me a kingdom of priests and a holy nation.
> —EXODUS 19:5–6

Under the new covenant, God raised up a new priesthood. "But
you are a chosen generation, a royal priesthood, a holy nation, His
own special people, that you may proclaim the praises of Him who
called you out of darkness into His marvelous light" (1 Pet. 2:9).

We struggle with the concept of being priests because we view
a priest as a religious person in a fancy robe doing religious activi-
ties. We do not see the priesthood as the most sacred intimate
intercourse with God Himself. We fail to see the priest as a royal,
kingly, God-chosen position. To minister unto God is not to perform some ministerial service; rather, it is to connect with and
touch the heart of God in the most intimate and personal way.
The priesthood is to behold and connect with the glory of God

and proclaim that revelation throughout eternity. The priesthood is the highest and most sacred calling, and as born-again believers we are called to be holy priests unto God.

We are called to this priesthood because we are one with the eternal High Priest, Jesus, who is "a priest forever, in the order of Melchizedek" (Heb. 7:17, MEV). As High Priest unto God, Jesus "obtained a more excellent ministry, because He is the mediator of a better covenant, which was established on better promises" (Heb. 8:6, MEV). "He at all times lives to make intercession for them" (Heb. 7:25, MEV).

Jesus as our High Priest leads us in ministry to the Father, forever connects us to the Father, and partners with us in the ministry of priesthood. "As He is, so are we in this world" (1 John 4:17, MEV). Jesus is a priest, and He is making us into a holy priesthood.

Our commissioning as priests is laid out in 1 Peter: "Coming to Him as to a living stone who is rejected by men, but chosen by God and precious, you also, as living stones, are being built up into a spiritual house as a holy priesthood to offer up spiritual sacrifices that are acceptable to God through Jesus Christ" (1 Pet. 2:4–5, MEV).

Peter says we are being built into a spiritual house, a holy priesthood, for a divine purpose. This purpose is to offer up to God spiritual sacrifices through Jesus Christ that are acceptable to God. Here is a great truth: Not everything we do is acceptable to God. Only our spiritual sacrifices through Jesus Christ are acceptable. Just because we slap Jesus' name on something or say we are doing it for God does not mean it is an acceptable sacrifice. The only things that are acceptable to God are those things that are done through Him, for Him, and by His empowerment.

We are God's house and are priests unto and for God. Only by the power and direction of the Holy Spirit can we offer acceptable sacrifices to God. Only as we yield our bodies, our worship, our works, and our giving to the Lord, for His glory, are they acceptable. Only that which is done through the Lord Jesus by the power of the Holy Spirit is an acceptable sacrifice.

We cannot be priests and offer acceptable sacrifices if we do things our way. We must follow the pattern laid out in Scripture and yield our hearts, minds, and bodies to the Holy Spirit. We are reminded in Hebrews 8:5 that we "serve in a sanctuary that is an example and shadow of the heavenly one, as Moses was instructed by God when he was about to make the tabernacle, 'See that you make all things according to the pattern shown you on the mountain'" (MEV).

Our focus must be on Him and for Him. When we look unto Jesus, we focus on who He is and what He is focused on. We align our hearts with the heart of God so we can offer service unto God as priests, holy and acceptable to Him. We are joint heirs with Christ as His bride, but we function as God's priests.

The concept of priesthood goes all the way back to Adam in the Garden of Eden. "There are significant parallels in the language used for Adam's duty in the Garden and the Levites' duty in the tabernacle. Just as God put Adam in the Garden to 'work and keep' it (Genesis 2:15), the Levites were told to 'work' and 'keep' the sanctuary of the tabernacle/temple (Numbers 3:7–8; 8:26; 18:5–6). The Hebrew עבד, *avad* ("*to work*") and שמר, *shamar* ("*to keep*") can also be translated "*serve/minister*" and "*guard*" respectively. And Yahweh God took the man and put him in the Garden of Eden to serve it and guard it [הַרְמֵשְׁלוּ הַרְבָעֶל] (Genesis 2:15)."[2]

We who are born again have been made a kingdom of priests. We have been given a priestly anointing, authority, and commission. To help us understand this, let's look at the Old Testament priest as a model foreshadowing what we are called to do.

1. Priests were set apart for God.

> And you shall be holy to Me, for I the LORD am holy, and have separated you from the peoples, that you should be Mine.
>
> —LEVITICUS 20:26

The priests were not to be wrapped up in worldly things. They knew they had special access to the presence of God, and that required a separation from unholy things. Only a separated life was an acceptable sacrifice.

> I appeal to you therefore, brethren, and beg of you in view of [all] the mercies of God, to make a decisive dedication of your bodies [presenting all your members and faculties] as a living sacrifice, holy (devoted, consecrated) and well pleasing to God, which is your reasonable (rational, intelligent) service and spiritual worship.
> —ROMANS 12:1, AMPC

2. Priests were given access to behold God in His glory. We see this played out repeatedly. Only those who honored God, revered Him, and feared Him had access to His manifested presence. Ezekiel 44 tells of the days following the Babylonian captivity when many of the priests allowed worldly practices and worship to be mixed with the worship of God. God released judgment on them. These compromising priests were no longer allowed to come before the presence of God to minister to Him.

> "Because they ministered to them before their idols and caused the house of Israel to fall into iniquity, therefore I have raised My hand in an oath against them," says the Lord GOD, "that they shall bear their iniquity. And they shall not come near Me to minister to Me as priest, nor come near any of My holy things, nor into the Most Holy Place; but they shall bear their shame and their abominations which they have committed. Nevertheless I will make them keep charge of the temple, for all its work, and for all that has to be done in it."
> —EZEKIEL 44:12–14

They were allowed to continue to minister to the people but were banned from accessing the holy place. They failed to guard the worship of God and keep it pure. They no longer served God but their own self-interest by doing things the people wanted.

They engaged in the idolatry of the day and incorporated it into the worship of God. History is repeating itself.

God is the same yesterday, today, and forever. The revelation that He loved us, washed us in His blood, and made us kings and priests should cause us to want to serve God and guard the worship of God. We have been given the right to enter the holy of holies to behold His glory. This should produce in us a consecration and separation from that which is contrary to God and His nature.

Hebrews 10:29 says, "How much more severe a punishment do you suppose he deserves, who has trampled under foot the Son of God, and has regarded the blood of the covenant that sanctified him to be a common thing, and has insulted the Spirit of grace?" (MEV).

3. Priests ate the bread, which speaks of divine revelation, and drank the cup, which speaks of deep covenant communion with God. They ministered to God and before God by engaging in communion with God. The worship of God—communing with Him in prayer and the Word—ministers to God. It brings God great delight and enjoyment when we spend time with Him to love and honor Him.

The priestly anointing gives us access to an intimate relationship with God, and it also places upon us the responsibility to teach the Word and the pure worship of God to the rest of humanity. We must do this by what we say and what we do. We are His ambassadors of reconciliation. "And whatever you do in word or deed, do all in the name of the Lord Jesus, giving thanks to God the Father through Him" (Col. 3:17, MEV).

4. Priests had an inheritance that no others had.

> The Levitical priests and all the tribe of Levi will not have any portion or inheritance with Israel. They must eat the offerings of the LORD made by fire and His portion. They will have no inheritance among their brothers. The LORD is their inheritance, just as He has said to them.
>
> —DEUTERONOMY 18:1–2, MEV

This incredible statement cannot be overstated. God Himself is the inheritance of the priests. All that God is and all that God has is given to the priesthood. God Himself and His glory were given to the priests. Paul says that you "were sealed with the promised Holy Spirit, who is the guarantee of our inheritance" (Eph. 1:13–14, MEV), and in verse 18 he prays "that the eyes of your understanding may be enlightened, that you may know what is the hope of His calling and what are the riches of the glory of His inheritance among the saints" (MEV).

Jesus, the firstborn Son and a priest forever, prays to His Father, "I have given them the glory which You gave Me, that they may be one even as We are one" (John 17:22, MEV). We are not focused on wealth, riches, power, or fame, for we have a greater inheritance. We are His inheritance, and He is ours. He has given us all things.

5. Priests were given authority and a commission to reveal God to the people and to reconcile people to God through the revelation of Christ. The priests were active in the ministry of reconciliation. They were commissioned to teach God's commands. This is explained in Ezekiel 44:23: "They shall teach My people the difference between the holy and profane, and cause them to discern between the unclean and the clean" (MEV).

Now, in the new covenant, God commissions us as priests.

> Now all things are of God, who has reconciled us to Himself through Jesus Christ, and has given us the ministry of reconciliation, that is, that God was in Christ reconciling the world to Himself, not imputing their trespasses to them, and has committed to us the word of reconciliation. Now then, we are ambassadors for Christ, as though God were pleading through us: we implore you on Christ's behalf, be reconciled to God.
>
> —2 CORINTHIANS 5:18–20

We are called to be the salt and light of the world. As priests we are called to serve and guard the worship and Word of God. We must be actively engaged in preaching, teaching, ministering, and sharing the gospel. When wickedness arises, we must speak up and declare the truth of the gospel. All of us who are born again are God's priests in this world.

The priesthood is not some religious institution. It is the very position Jesus has taken as fully man and fully God to minister unto and on behalf of His Father. Jesus is a priest forever. He loved us and washed us so that we can be in this eternal divine partnership with Him. We can be a kingdom of priests. We can be like Him. We will be priests forever.

Jesus, as the firstborn from the dead, is bringing many sons unto glory. He loved us and washed us for a divine purpose. He has made us His most holy priests to minister unto the Father and on behalf of Him.

> And have made us kings and priests to our God; and we shall reign on the earth.
>
> —REVELATION 5:10

These descriptions of Jesus reveal that He focuses on who He is and the age to come. He loved us and washed us because He wanted a people, a bride, with whom He would share all of Himself. He wants us to partner with Him in all things as His bride who is a kingdom of priests. He has called us to be like Him in all things.

We are His priests now, and we will be priests in the age to come. We are ministers unto God and on behalf of God unto the peoples of the earth.

> Blessed and holy is he who has part in the first resurrection. Over such the second death has no power, but they shall be priests of God and of Christ, and shall reign with Him a thousand years.
>
> —REVELATION 20:6

We will be God's priests during the millennial reign. There will be humans on the earth. They will grow, have babies, marry, work, live, and build lives here on the earth. We who are the bride of

Christ, the ones who are part of the first resurrection, will have resurrected bodies. We will rule and reign with Christ here on the earth for a thousand years. We will assist the Lord in administering justice and His kingdom on the earth. We will be in full partnership with Jesus as priests forever.

In this incredible love story called the gospel, Jesus loved us and shed His blood to rescue His bride so that He could share all that He is and has with us. He has forgiven and redeemed us and makes us like Himself, a priest. We are a royal priesthood to love, worship, and minister to God the Father and declare the praises of God to all generations now and forevermore. Therefore, in "whatever you do, do it heartily, as for the Lord and not for men, knowing that from the Lord you will receive the reward of the inheritance. For you serve the Lord Christ" (Col. 3:23–24, MEV).

Prayer

Father, make me a royal priesthood. Teach me how to offer You acceptable sacrifices that are holy and pleasing to You. Bring me ever closer in the deepest intimacy with Your heart. Fill my heart with the worship of heaven, and anoint me to declare Your praises to and for You throughout the earth. I choose to be in full partnership with Jesus as a priest forever. My eyes are upon You. In Jesus' holy name, amen.

Day 10
THE CLOUDS OF HEAVEN

Behold, He is coming with clouds, and every eye will see Him, even they who pierced Him. And all the tribes of the earth will mourn because of Him. Even so, Amen.
—REVELATION 1:7

THIS DECLARATION THAT Jesus is coming with clouds is unbelievably prophetically significant. This is not simply an image of Jesus riding on His horse on a big puffy cloud like we see in many pictures.

"The clouds" speaks of the second coming of Christ to execute judgment upon the Antichrist and to rule and reign on the earth.

> Then the sign of the Son of Man will appear in heaven, and then all the tribes of the earth will mourn, and they will see the Son of Man coming on the clouds of heaven with power and great glory.
>
> —MATTHEW 24:30

This event will be so full of power and glory that those on the earth who have rejected Christ will mourn because of the manifestation of Jesus. The Book of Revelation describes this manifestation as spectacular and terrifying:

> I looked when He opened the sixth seal, and behold, there was a great earthquake; and the sun became black as sackcloth of hair, and the moon became like blood. And the stars of heaven fell to the earth, as a fig tree drops its late figs when it is shaken by a mighty wind. Then the sky receded as a scroll when it is rolled up, and every mountain and island was moved out of its place. And the kings of the earth, the great men, the rich men, the commanders, the mighty men, every slave and every free man, hid themselves in the caves and in the rocks of the

71

mountains, and said to the mountains and rocks, "Fall
on us and hide us from the face of Him who sits on the
throne and from the wrath of the Lamb! For the great day
of His wrath has come, and who is able to stand?"

—REVELATION 6:12–17

This is the second coming of Christ. Matthew tells us when
this event will take place: "For as the lightning comes from the
east and flashes to the west, so will be the coming of the Son of
Man. Wherever the carcass is, there the eagles will be gathered
together. Immediately after the tribulation of those days, the sun
will be darkened, the moon will not give its light; the stars will fall
from heaven, and the powers of the heavens will be shaken" (Matt.
24:27–29, MEV).

These verses describe the great tribulation talked about in
Matthew 24:21: "For then will be great tribulation, such as has not
happened since the beginning of the world until now, no, nor ever
shall be" (MEV).

The event of Jesus coming with clouds is "immediately after the
tribulation of those days" (Matt. 24:29, MEV). Joel tells us, "The
sun shall be turned to darkness, and the moon to blood, before
the great and awesome day of the LORD comes" (Joel 2:31, ESV).

The great day of the LORD is near; it is near and hastens
quickly. The noise of the day of the LORD is bitter; there
the mighty men shall cry out. That day is a day of wrath.

—ZEPHANIAH 1:14–15

John would have known what this was referring to. The Jews
had long looked for the coming of the Messiah, when He would
take over rulership of all the nations of the world. This image of
coming with the clouds points directly to the prophetic vision of
Daniel in chapter 7.

I was watching in the night visions, and behold, One
like the Son of Man, coming with the clouds of heaven!
He came to the Ancient of Days, and they brought Him

> near before Him. Then to Him was given dominion and
> glory and a kingdom, that all peoples, nations, and lan-
> guages should serve Him. His dominion is an everlasting
> dominion, which shall not pass away, and His kingdom
> the one which shall not be destroyed.
>
> —DANIEL 7:13–14

This prophecy was so dynamic. A man was going to sit on the throne of God. This man, Jesus, would go to the Father, the Ancient of Days, and receive the power and dominion over all. The Son of Man coming with the clouds invokes the image of the Messiah. This is why the Pharisees responded with such anger when Jesus said, "'Hereafter you will see the Son of Man seated at the right hand of Power and coming on the clouds of heaven.' Then the high priest tore his clothes, saying, 'He has uttered blasphemy. What further need do we have for witnesses? See, now you have heard His blasphemy. What do you think?' They answered, 'He is guilty unto death'" (Matt. 26:64–66, MEV).

Why did the Pharisees condemn Jesus to death? Because He dared declare Himself the Messiah spoken of by Daniel the prophet. He declared that He was the One coming on the clouds of heaven, the One to whom God the Father would hand all authority and who would rule forever.

Also understand that the context of Daniel's prophecy was the season of the rise of the Antichrist. He spoke of the Antichrist's kingdom:

> He shall speak pompous words against the Most High,
> shall persecute the saints of the Most High, and shall
> intend to change times and law. Then the saints shall be
> given into his hand for a time and times and half a time.
> But the court shall be seated, and they shall take away his
> dominion, to consume and destroy it forever.
>
> —DANIEL 7:25–26

When we see this description of Jesus coming with clouds, we see the victorious King coming to execute judgment upon the

Antichrist and his kingdom. We see the Mighty One of Israel returning to destroy all wickedness and establish the kingdom of heaven on the earth.

The clouds also speak of God's visible manifested glory.

> Now the LORD descended in the cloud and stood with him there, and proclaimed the name of the LORD. And the LORD passed before him and proclaimed, "The LORD, the LORD God, merciful and gracious, longsuffering, and abounding in goodness and truth, keeping mercy for thousands, forgiving iniquity and transgression and sin, by no means clearing the guilty, visiting the iniquity of the fathers upon the children and the children's children to the third and the fourth generation."
>
> —EXODUS 34:5–7

> Then the cloud covered the tabernacle of meeting, and the glory of the LORD filled the tabernacle. And Moses was not able to enter the tabernacle of meeting, because the cloud rested above it, and the glory of the LORD filled the tabernacle.
>
> —EXODUS 40:34–35

The clouds are manifested in response to the worship and prayers of God's people.

We must understand this part. God's glory and end-time purposes on the earth will not be fulfilled apart from us but in response to our worship and prayers. We are partners with Jesus through intercession in releasing the power and glory of God upon the earth.

> Then another angel, having a golden censer, came and stood at the altar. He was given much incense, that he should offer it with the prayers of all the saints upon the golden altar which was before the throne. And the smoke of the incense, with the prayers of the saints, ascended before God from the angel's hand. Then the angel took the censer, filled it with fire from the altar, and threw it

to the earth. And there were noises, thunderings, lightnings, and an earthquake.

—REVELATION 8:3–5

The burning of incense is associated with the prayers of the saints throughout the Bible. The Old Testament called the smoke from the incense a cloud. "And he shall put the incense on the fire before the LORD, that the cloud of the incense may cover the mercy seat that is over the testimony" (Lev. 16:13, MEV).

We see the angel take the censer filled with the prayers of the saints and ignite it with the fire from the altar of God. He then threw it back to the earth. This is an image of the divine connection between God's end-time events and the prayers of the saints. We are going to be in full partnership with Jesus to pray in and release the events that will ultimately result in the conquering of the Antichrist and the establishment of God's throne upon the earth. What an amazing privilege.

The church will be completely aligned with Jesus under the power of the Holy Spirit. Then God the Father will release events in response to the intercession of the saints.

> And the Spirit and the bride say, "Come!" And let him who hears say, "Come!" And let him who thirsts come. Whoever desires, let him take the water of life freely.
>
> —REVELATION 22:17

The Lord Jesus is going to return with the clouds of heaven. These clouds are the result of the prayers of the saints. Let that sink in. Our prayers mixed with the fire of God's altar will release clouds of God's glory in heaven upon which Jesus will ride when He returns to earth to conquer the Antichrist.

> And it came to pass, when the priests came out of the holy place, that the cloud filled the house of the LORD, so that the priests could not continue ministering because of the cloud; for the glory of the LORD filled the house of the LORD.
>
> —1 KINGS 8:10–11

When the priest (who we now are) ministered to God in worship and intercession, the glory cloud of God was manifested. Worship and intercession intwined together will release the cloud that carries the glory. We will see more of this in the days ahead.

The clouds, the glory of God, and the worship and intercession of the saints are all connected. An end-time prayer and worship anointing has already begun. It will fill the church and result in the glory of God filling the earth. This mighty prayer and worship anointing on God's people will ultimately result in Jesus' second coming to earth. He will ride with the clouds of heaven to execute vengeance on the nations and judgment on the people to bring righteousness, justice, and a kingdom that never dies.

> Let the high praises of God be in their mouth [worship], and a two-edged sword in their hand [intercession with the Word], to execute vengeance on the nations, and punishments on the peoples; to bind their kings with chains, and their nobles with fetters of iron; to execute on them the written judgment—this honor have all His saints. Praise the LORD!
>
> —Psalm 149:6–9

Worship and intercession anointings are connected to the end-time judgments of God. We have the honor of releasing the power and glory of God through our worship and intercession to judge the wicked and fulfill God's end-time plan. Jesus our Bridegroom is coming back riding on the clouds of heaven to be eternally joined with His bride, whom He has made a kingdom of priests. As priests, through prayer and worship, empowered by the Holy Spirit, we have been crying out for His return: "The Spirit and the bride say, 'Come.' Let him who hears say, 'Come.' Let him who is thirsty come. Let him who desires take the water of life freely" (Rev. 22:17, MEV).

Our prayers and worship will release the manifestation of the cloud of glory upon which Jesus will return.

Meditate upon Daniel's revelation of the One who comes with the clouds of heaven:

> One like the Son of Man, coming with the clouds of heaven! He came to the Ancient of Days, and they brought Him near before Him. Then to Him was given dominion and glory and a kingdom, that all peoples, nations, and languages should serve Him. His dominion is an everlasting dominion, which shall not pass away, and His kingdom the one which shall not be destroyed.
>
> —DANIEL 7:13–14

Prayer

Father, anoint me with this end-time prayer and worship anointing. Let my praise and intercession fill the heavens with clouds of glory. Place upon me the mantle of prayer and the spirit of worship that I may fulfill Your eternal purpose for my life to declare the praises of God. Fill me with hope and expectation of Jesus' soon return, and deliver me from every distraction. O Lord, send Your glory once again that the world may see Your beauty. In Jesus' holy name, amen.

Day 11
THE PATIENCE OF JESUS CHRIST

I, John, both your brother and companion in the tribulation and kingdom and patience of Jesus Christ, was...in the Spirit on the Lord's Day.
—REVELATION 1:9–10

THERE ARE MANY descriptions of Jesus in the Book of Revelation. Although some scholars may not include the patience of Jesus in their list, I think it was placed in verse 9 for a very specific divine purpose. Since these revelations of Jesus are given to prepare us for the most intense season the world will ever go through, the need for the patience of Jesus is even more important now than ever.

The word *patient* in the Greek means patient endurance. It speaks of a steadfastness and fortitude to withstand stress and hardships, especially inner fortitude.

> **hupomonē**; from 5278; a remaining behind, a patient enduring: endurance.[1]

In his book *Word Studies in the New Testament*, Martin R. Vincent writes, "*Remaining behind* or *staying, to wait*. Not merely endurance of the inevitable, for Christ could have relieved himself of his sufferings...but the heroic, brave patience with which a Christian not only *bears* but *contends*."[2]

> Now may the Lord direct your hearts into the love of God and into the patience of Christ.
> —2 THESSALONIANS 3:5

We are called to patiently endure, to faithfully press into God even while experiencing lack of cooperation and many annoying issues like lack of finances and appreciation, health troubles, disappointments, and problems with relationships. Yes, we are called to serve God in the face of frustrating circumstances. However, most of the issues that cause us to back off from intensely pressing into God and His service are small things, but the piling on of those small things becomes our undoing.

The true love of God produces the patience of Christ in us. This patient endurance is an inner supernatural strength that causes us to overcome and press hard into God despite our circumstances. Human strength, a strong will, and determination will not be enough in the days ahead. We must see that Jesus, as fully man here on the earth, through the power of the Holy Spirit, had the power of patient endurance.

Jesus is about to reveal to John the intensity of the events to come. For this reason, John's attention is drawn to the powerful fruit of the Holy Spirit called patient endurance, or long-suffering.

Paul preached of this kind of endurance immediately after he was stoned in Lystra.

> Then Jews from Antioch and Iconium came there; and having persuaded the multitudes, they stoned Paul and dragged him out of the city, supposing him to be dead. However, when the disciples gathered around him, he rose up and went into the city. And the next day he departed with Barnabas to Derbe. And when they had preached the gospel to that city and made many disciples, they returned to Lystra, Iconium, and Antioch, strengthening the souls of the disciples, exhorting them to continue in the faith, and saying, "We must through many tribulations enter the kingdom of God."
>
> —ACTS 14:19–22

Have you ever wondered how these early saints endured so much and kept faithful when it seems like today it's so easy to quit, back away, and even fall away from Christ? The impartation of the manifestation of patient endurance came from seeing Jesus as He is. Hebrews 12:1–2 says, "And let us run with endurance the race God has set before us. We do this by keeping our eyes on Jesus" (NLT).

As we keep our eyes on Jesus and what He is focused on, He imparts to us the amazing strength and power called patient endurance. The secret to this power being released in and through us is the opposite of what we think. We expect God to fill us with an emotion of strength where we charge out every day like a warrior running to battle ready to conquer anything that comes against us. The painful truth is that God reveals and releases this power called patient endurance in the midst of trouble and suffering.

Suffering causes this power to be manifested. It doesn't usually happen before the battle but in the midst of the battle as we look to Him.

> My brethren, count it all joy when you fall into various trials, knowing that *the testing of your faith produces patience.* But let patience have its perfect work, that you may be perfect and complete, lacking nothing.
> —James 1:2–4, emphasis added

> And not only that, but we also glory in tribulations, knowing *that tribulation produces perseverance* [patience]; and perseverance, character; and character, hope. Now hope does not disappoint, because the love of God has been poured out in our hearts by the Holy Spirit who was given to us.
> —Romans 5:3–5, emphasis added

Power is manifested in and through us when we suffer. So much of modern church teaches us that Jesus came to deliver us from problems. We expect continual financial provision, perfect health, great relationships, and favor with God and men. We have not taught the church that suffering is not only an expected part of the Christian experience but is also the place where an amazing supernatural gift is released in and through us: the patience of Jesus.

This patience is the key to unlocking the greatest of our heavenly rewards. These rewards are given to those who overcome, to those who endure until the end.

Romans 2:6–7 says that God "'will render to each one according to his deeds': eternal life to those who by patient continuance in doing good seek for glory, honor, and immortality."

The revelation knowledge of God that we gain as we behold Him as He is fills us with the wisdom and spiritual understanding that produces patience and long-suffering.

> For this reason we also, since the day we heard it, do not cease to pray for you, and to ask that you may be filled with the knowledge of His will in all wisdom and spiritual understanding; that you may walk worthy of the Lord, fully pleasing Him, being fruitful in every good work and increasing in the knowledge of God; strengthened with all might, according to His glorious power, *for all patience and longsuffering with joy.*
> —COLOSSIANS 1:9–11, EMPHASIS ADDED

In our battles and struggles, the resurrected life that raised Christ from the dead will flow in and through our bodies. The seed of Christ is inside of you. The Spirit that raised Jesus from the dead will quicken and strengthen you. The strength is released in the suffering, not apart from it. Paul taught this so powerfully in 2 Corinthians 4:6–11:

> For it is the God who commanded light to shine out of darkness, who has shone in our hearts to give the light of the knowledge of the glory of God in the face of Jesus Christ. But we have this treasure in earthen vessels, that the excellence of the power may be of God and not of us. We are hard-pressed on every side, yet not crushed; we are perplexed, but not in despair; persecuted, but not forsaken; struck down, but not destroyed—always carrying about in the body the dying of the Lord Jesus, that the life of Jesus also may be manifested in our body. For we who

live are always delivered to death for Jesus' sake, that the
life of Jesus also may be manifested in our mortal flesh.

The Amplified Bible, Classic Edition has interesting wording for
verse 11: "For we who live are constantly [experiencing] being handed
over to death for Jesus' sake, that the [resurrection] life of Jesus also
may be evidenced through our flesh which is liable to death."

Then, in verses 13 and 14, Paul speaks of our confession of faith.
In the context of intense suffering he declares, "We have the same
spirit of faith. As it is written, 'I believed, and therefore I have
spoken.' So we also believe and therefore speak, knowing that He
who raised the Lord Jesus will also raise us through Jesus and will
present us with you" (MEV).

The spirit of faith recognizes that when we endure suffering,
struggles, battles, and hardships while looking unto Jesus, we
experience the glory and power of God in and through our bodies.

Jesus points us to the end of the age, the season we have now
entered, the days preceding His return. He shows us the need of
this patience to stay strong with Him.

> Nation will rise against nation, and kingdom against
> kingdom. And there will be great earthquakes in various
> places, and famines and pestilences; and there will be
> fearful sights and great signs from heaven. But before all
> these things, they will lay their hands on you and perse-
> cute you, delivering you up to the synagogues and prisons.
> You will be brought before kings and rulers for My name's
> sake. But it will turn out for you as an occasion for tes-
> timony. Therefore settle it in your hearts not to meditate
> beforehand on what you will answer; for I will give you a
> mouth and wisdom which all your adversaries will not be
> able to contradict or resist. You will be betrayed even by
> parents and brothers, relatives and friends; and they will
> put some of you to death. And you will be hated by all for
> My name's sake. But not a hair of your head shall be lost.
> *By your patience possess your souls.*
>   —LUKE 21:10–19, EMPHASIS ADDED

"By your patience possess your souls." The word *possess* means "obtain, acquire, win. *The acquisition of something of significance...* it refers to a person acquiring material gain or earnings."

This patience of Jesus will give you the ability to gain control of your mind, will, and emotions.

This patience of Jesus is available to all as we keep our eyes focused on Him and what He is focused on. Meditate on these words from the writer of Hebrews:

> Just think of Him Who endured from sinners such grievous opposition and bitter hostility against Himself [reckon up and consider it all in comparison with your trials], so that you may not grow weary or exhausted, losing heart and relaxing and fainting in your minds.
> —HEBREWS 12:3, AMPC

As we behold Jesus and His patient endurance, we too are strengthened to continue in well doing and not grow weary and faint in our minds. As He is, so are we in this world.

Prayer

Father, grant me the patient endurance of Jesus. Fill me with the fruit of long-suffering. As I go through the challenges and struggles of this life, let the resurrection life of Jesus also be manifest in my body. I cannot do this with my own human effort, but my eyes are upon You. Hold me, carry me, strengthen me, and empower me for every good work. I trust that You are able to keep that which I have committed to You, and He who began a good work in me shall bring it unto completion. In Jesus' holy name, amen.

Day 12
A VOICE LIKE A TRUMPET

I was in the Spirit on the Lord's Day, and I heard
behind me a loud voice, as of a trumpet.
—REVELATION 1:10

THESE DESCRIPTIONS OF Jesus reveal His nature, His heart, and His ways. This description may make it seem like He has a loud voice, but this passage of Scripture is so much more powerful than that. Whenever we are studying the Word, we must remember a rule of hermeneutics called the law of first mention. "The Law of First Mention may be said to be the principle that requires one to go to that portion of the Scriptures where a doctrine is mentioned for the first time and to study the first occurrence of the same in order to get the fundamental inherent meaning of that doctrine."[1]

The first place a trumpet is mentioned, it is connected to God revealing Himself to the children of Israel in the wilderness.

> When the trumpet sounds long, they shall come near the mountain.
>
> —EXODUS 19:13

> Then it came to pass on the third day, in the morning, that there were thunderings and lightnings, and a thick cloud on the mountain; and the sound of the trumpet was very loud, so that all the people who were in the camp trembled.
>
> —EXODUS 19:16

> And when the blast of the trumpet sounded long and became louder and louder, Moses spoke, and God answered him by voice. Then the LORD came down upon Mount Sinai, on the top of the mountain. And the LORD called Moses to the top of the mountain, and Moses went up.
>
> —EXODUS 19:19–20

The Israelites did not blow a trumpet. The sound of the trumpet came from God on the mountain. The instruction of God was when the trumpet sound was long, His people were to come near to Him. The sound of the trumpet is a call from God for us to come up to where He is. It is a call for us to come near: "And the LORD called Moses to the top of the mountain, and Moses went up" (Exod. 19:20).

God was about to reveal Himself in a new dimension.

When John heard the voice of Jesus like a trumpet, it spoke of God calling us up to a new revelation and a new dimension of relationship with Him. The voice of God as a trumpet was also revealed to foreshadow heavenly things in the instruments God commanded to be made for the tabernacle in the wilderness. The sound of the trumpet was associated with God calling His people to Himself.

> Make two silver trumpets for yourself; you shall make them of hammered work; you shall use them for calling the congregation and for directing the movement of the camps. When they blow both of them, all the congregation shall gather before you at the door of the tabernacle of meeting.
>
> —NUMBERS 10:2–3

The door of the tabernacle is where God appeared to Moses.

> And it came to pass, when Moses entered the tabernacle, that the pillar of cloud descended and stood at the door of the tabernacle, and the LORD talked with Moses. All the people saw the pillar of cloud standing at the tabernacle door....So the LORD spoke to Moses face to face, as a man speaks to his friend.
>
> —EXODUS 33:9–11

When the voice of the Lord is as a trumpet, it is God calling us to *come close* to Him because He wants to speak to us and reveal Himself.

What a glorious description of Jesus! John understood by this manifestation of the voice of God as a loud trumpet that God was about to speak to him as He would speak with a friend. God was about to reveal His glory, majesty, and plans to John in a new dimension.

We see this calling up to God in Revelation chapter 4: "After this I looked. And there was an open door in heaven. The first voice I heard *was like a trumpet speaking* with me, saying, 'Come up here, and I will show you things which must take place after this'" (Rev. 4:1, MEV, emphasis added).

Jesus called John up to heaven. He first saw the throne room of God and then was shown the end-time events that would take place.

This description of Jesus is telling us that the end-time saints will operate in great prophetic revelation. God will release the greatest manifestation of the revelation of Himself to the generation immediately preceding the return of Christ. "Come up here, and I will show you things which must take place after this" (Rev. 4:1, MEV).

The loud voice as a trumpet will declare the release of God's end-time judgments. These things will happen simultaneously.

> And I looked, and I heard an angel flying through the midst of heaven, saying with a loud voice, "Woe, woe, woe to the inhabitants of the earth, because of the remaining blasts of the trumpet of the three angels who are about to sound!"
>
> —REVELATION 8:13

There will be an unprecedented release of wickedness and darkness upon the earth in the days ahead. We are already seeing it manifest. However, in the midst of this darkness and evil spreading throughout the earth like a swarm of locusts, God will release a trumpet blast. He will call His people to draw closer to Him than at any time in history. God's people (His bride) will consecrate themselves, separate themselves, and pray with a new intensity that will release the greatest prophetic anointing that the world has ever known.

We see this in the Book of Joel. Joel chapter 2 is all about the last days. There are multiple soundings of the trumpets. The first blast of the trumpet will warn the world that the time of the end of the age has come. This will be a warning of judgment and a final call to repentance.

> Blow a trumpet in Zion; sound an alarm on my holy mountain! Let all the inhabitants of the land tremble, for the day of the LORD is coming; it is near, a day of darkness and gloom, a day of clouds and thick darkness! Like blackness there is spread upon the mountains a great and powerful people; their like has never been before, nor will be again after them through the years of all generations.
>
> —JOEL 2:1–2, ESV

> "Yet even now," declares the LORD, "return to me with all your heart, with fasting, with weeping, and with mourning; and rend your hearts and not your garments." Return to the LORD your God, for he is gracious and merciful, slow to anger, and abounding in steadfast love; and he relents over disaster.
>
> —JOEL 2:12–13, ESV

The next trumpet blast will call God's people to draw close to Him for repentance and intercession.

> Blow the trumpet in Zion, consecrate a fast, call a sacred assembly; gather the people, sanctify the congregation, assemble the elders, gather the children and nursing babes; let the bridegroom go out from his chamber, and the bride from her dressing room. Let the priests, who minister to the LORD, weep between the porch and the altar; let them say, "Spare Your people, O LORD, and do not give Your heritage to reproach, that the nations

should rule over them. Why should they say among the
peoples, 'Where is their God?'"

—JOEL 2:15–17

God responds to this prayer and repentance by His people with
amazing promises to deliver and pour out His Spirit in abundant
measures. He will forgive us, and then He will open the floodgates
of heaven like never before.

> The LORD will answer and say to His people, "Behold, I
> will send you grain and new wine and oil, and you will be
> satisfied by them; I will no longer make you a reproach
> among the nations."

—JOEL 2:19

This all culminates with the passage we all know so well, the
promise of an outpouring of the prophetic anointing that will
sweep the whole world and cause the greatest revelation and manifestation of God to be displayed.

> And it shall come to pass afterward that I will pour out
> My Spirit on all flesh; your sons and your daughters shall
> prophesy, your old men shall dream dreams, your young
> men shall see visions. And also on My menservants and
> on My maidservants I will pour out My Spirit in those
> days.

—JOEL 2:28–29

When we see Jesus as He truly is, we will pray, worship, and
preach the gospel. There will be a final undeniable display of the
glory of God on and through His church.

> Arise, shine; for your light has come! And the glory of the
> LORD is risen upon you. For behold, the darkness shall
> cover the earth, and deep darkness the people; but the
> LORD will arise over you, and His glory will be seen upon
> you.

—ISAIAH 60:1–2

This will result in what I believe will be the greatest harvest of souls in history.

> The Gentiles shall come to your light, and kings to the brightness of your rising.
> —ISAIAH 60:3

When you see Jesus with a loud voice as a trumpet, realize this is the voice of God calling His people to come close to Him. This is His voice warning the unbelievers of impending judgment. Ever desiring mercy, God will shake everything that can be shaken while extending His gracious hand of mercy and forgiveness. The trumpet will call everyone to Him.

> If a trumpet is blown in a city, will not the people be afraid? If there is calamity in a city, will not the LORD have done it? Surely the Lord GOD does nothing, unless He reveals His secret to His servants the prophets. A lion has roared! Who will not fear? The Lord GOD has spoken! Who can but prophesy?
> —AMOS 3:6–8

The final manifestation of the Lord's voice as a trumpet will be when the heaven splits open and the Lord returns to take us up with Him when He takes rulership of the earth. The final trumpet calls His people to Himself in the rapture and releases the final wrath of the Lamb upon the wicked.

> For the Lord Himself will descend from heaven with a shout, with the voice of an archangel, and with the trumpet of God. And the dead in Christ will rise first. Then we who are alive and remain shall be caught up together with them in the clouds to meet the Lord in the air. And thus we shall always be with the Lord. Therefore comfort one another with these words.
> —1 THESSALONIANS 4:16–18

Then the seventh angel sounded: And there were loud voices in heaven, saying, "The kingdoms of this world have become the kingdoms of our Lord and of His Christ, and He shall reign forever and ever!" And the twenty-four elders who sat before God on their thrones fell on their faces and worshiped God, saying:…"The nations were angry, and Your wrath has come, and the time of the dead, that they should be judged, and that You should reward Your servants the prophets and the saints, and those who fear Your name, small and great, and should destroy those who destroy the earth."

—REVELATION 11:15–18

The loud voice of Jesus as a trumpet is calling us to come close as He releases deeper revelation of Himself. It warns of coming judgment through a last-days prophetic anointing that will culminate in the second coming of Christ.

Prayer

Father, teach me to hear the voice of Jesus as a trumpet. I choose to respond to Your calling me up into a higher and deeper revelation of You. Fill my mouth with the voice of the Almighty to proclaim Your words in these last days. Bring me into the manifestation of Your glory and help me walk in all Your ways. In Jesus' holy name, amen.

Day 13
THE ALPHA AND THE OMEGA

I was in the Spirit on the Lord's Day, and I
heard behind me a loud voice, as of a trumpet,
saying, "I am the Alpha and the Omega."
—REVELATION 1:10–11

EVERY DESCRIPTION HAS powerful revelation and great importance in God's unfolding of the most amazing love story of all
time. These key truths will strengthen us in the evil days in which we
find ourselves. The One who loves us is the Alpha and Omega. This
simple phrase is probably one of the most important in the Bible, but
it's hard for us to get our finite minds around the truth of it.

Most descriptions of God are distinctly Hebraic, but this one is
not. This would have caught John's attention, being a Jew. "As the
first letter of the [Greek] alphabet, Alpha as a Greek numeral came
to represent the number 1." Both as a symbol and a term, Alpha "is
used to refer to the 'first,' or 'primary,' or 'principal' (most significant) occurrence or status of a thing."[1]

When Jesus declares Himself the Alpha, He is saying that He
is the first, the primary, the most significant. He is above and has
the highest status of all, whether Jew or Greek.

It is amazing that in the Book of Revelation, God the Father
only speaks twice, and both times He declares Himself the Alpha
and Omega.

The Greek letter omega is the final letter. It means "the extreme
or final part: end."[2]

God is saying that He is the first and foremost above everyone
and everything. He is the extreme end of all things, and He exists
in everything in between. Jesus declares this same title at the
beginning and again at the end of the Book of Revelation.

> And behold, I am coming quickly, and My reward is with
> Me, to give to every one according to his work. I am the
> Alpha and the Omega, the Beginning and the End, the
> First and the Last.
>
> —REVELATION 22:12–13

Jesus is before all and after all. He was there *before* the beginning and will be there *after* the end. He is the capstone of all time,
space, and dimension. He is before and after.

> In the beginning was the Word, and the Word was with
> God, and the Word was God. He was in the beginning
> with God. All things were made through Him, and
> without Him nothing was made that was made.
>
> —JOHN 1:1–3

Jesus was in the beginning, and everything that was made
was created by and through Him. Nothing exists that He did not
create, and He sustains all of it. He is absolutely in total and complete control, for He was before the beginning, and He is after the
end. He controls all and everything in between.

> By the word of the LORD the heavens were made, and all
> the host of them by the breath of His mouth. He gathers
> the waters of the sea together as a heap; He lays up the
> deep in storehouses. Let all the earth fear the LORD; let all
> the inhabitants of the world stand in awe of Him. For He
> spoke, and it was done; He commanded, and it stood fast.
>
> —PSALM 33:6–9

No matter how much it seems like evil is winning, God has it
all under total control.

> The LORD brings the counsel of the nations to nothing;
> He makes the plans of the peoples of no effect. The
> counsel of the LORD stands forever, the plans of His heart
> to all generations.
>
> —PSALM 33:10–11

No matter what power of wickedness seems to stand against God and His holy servants, God's Word, plans, and purposes will be completed. This love story will have the happiest of endings.

In the days we are entering, it will seem at times as if evil is winning. When woke culture, the LGBTQ agenda, the sexualization of our children, and the demonizing of Christian values all seem to be taking over, Jesus is saying to us, "The LORD looks from heaven; He sees all the sons of men. From the place of His dwelling He looks on all the inhabitants of the earth; He fashions their hearts individually; He considers all their works. No king is saved by the multitude of an army; a mighty man is not delivered by great strength....Behold, the eye of the LORD is on those who fear Him, on those who hope in His mercy, to deliver their soul from death, and to keep them alive in famine" (Ps. 33:13–19).

There is great inner power and strength that fills us as we focus on Jesus as the Alpha and Omega. He and He alone is preeminent above and over all things.

> He is the image of the invisible God, the firstborn over all creation. For by Him all things were created that are in heaven and that are on earth, visible and invisible, whether thrones or dominions or principalities or powers. All things were created through Him and for Him. And He is before all things, and in Him all things consist. And He is the head of the body, the church, who is the beginning, the firstborn from the dead, that in all things He may have the preeminence.
>
> —COLOSSIANS 1:15–18

His power over darkness is not like what is portrayed in the movies where good barely overcomes evil. The reality is that Jesus is so far above and over the powers of evil that triumphing over evil is as nothing to Him. I love Isaiah 40 because it encapsulates this truth so fully. Isaiah 40 is an end-time prophecy. It clearly is speaking of when Jesus will return in all His power and glory to face off against the kingdoms of this world and the Antichrist. The prophet Isaiah starts by saying the following in verse 10:

> Behold, the Lord GOD shall come with a strong hand, and His arm shall rule for Him; behold, His reward is with Him, and His work before Him.
> —ISAIAH 40:10

Notice the similarity of this prophecy with the apostle John's prophecy of Jesus in Revelation 22:12–13: "Look, I am coming soon! My reward is with Me to give to each one according to his work. I am the Alpha and the Omega, the Beginning and the End, the First and the Last" (MEV). Isaiah also declares that in the last days, Jesus will "feed His flock like a shepherd; He shall gather the lambs with His arm, and carry them in His bosom, and shall gently lead those that are with young" (Isa. 40:11, MEV).

What a beautiful picture of Jesus coming back for His bride to gently gather us and protect us.

Isaiah then begins to lay out the case for how utterly transcendent and powerful God is.

> Who has measured the waters in the hollow of His hand, measured heaven with a span?
> —ISAIAH 40:12

God measures the universe with the width of His hand. In a sermon called "Jesus, Our Magnificent Obsession," Mike Bickle says, "The sun is a million miles in diameter. That's a big sun! You can fit a million earths into the space of the sun. The sun isn't one of the big stars in our galaxy. It's kind of a medium star. You could fit a million earths into that one space. The surface is two million degrees hot. Catch this: the energy the sun releases...is the equivalent of 100 *billion* hydrogen bombs per second....That's how much energy is coming off the sun, 100 billion hydrogen bombs every second....There are 100 million galaxies. The Milky Way is one."[3]

The radius of the known universe is over 45 billion light-years.

One light-year is about 5.8 trillion miles, the distance light travels in one Earth year. The known universe is 45 billion light-years in distance! The One who loves you created this universe and measures it with the span of His hand.

He also knows every speck of dust, "and calculated the dust of the earth in a measure" (Isa. 40:12, MEV). He is fully aware of every atom, every cell, and every speck of dust.

Here is another excerpt from Mike Bickle: "There's great complexity in a cell—in the tiniest bacteria. The cell of the tiniest bacteria is made up of 100 billion atoms. One cell of bacteria contains 100 billion atoms. Catch this: this cell has enough information to fill up the thirty volumes of the Encyclopedia Britannica. All thirty volumes could be filled up with the information in every cell....It's mindboggling. My point is, this is who He is. He's the Alpha and the Omega."[4] Jesus created all this and is fully aware of everything. This is Jesus. This is who we love and who is in control, and He is coming back.

Isaiah then addresses the power of the nations and leaders. When we feel overwhelmed by evil leaders and corporations, and wickedness on every side, we must remember:

> Behold, the nations are as a drop in a bucket, and are counted as the small dust on the scales; look, He lifts up the isles as a very little thing....All nations before Him are as nothing, and they are counted by Him less than nothing and worthless.
>
> —ISAIAH 40:15–17

The focus then turns to what we should be meditating on—God and His awesome power and glory—and that we should be strengthened through this knowledge of the One who loves us.

> Have you not known? Have you not heard? Has it not been told you from the beginning? Have you not understood from the foundations of the earth? It is He who sits above the circle of the earth, and its inhabitants are like grasshoppers, who stretches out the heavens like a

curtain, and spreads them out like a tent to dwell in. He
brings the princes to nothing; He makes the judges of the
earth useless....When He will also blow on them, and
they will wither, and the whirlwind will take them away
like stubble....Lift up your eyes on high, and see who
has created these things....Why do you say, O Jacob, and
speak, O Israel: "My way is hidden from the LORD, and
my just claim is passed over by my God"?
                                —ISAIAH 40:21–24, 26–27

When it seems like evil and trouble are on every side, just
remember who your God is. He is attentive to your prayers, even
when it seems like He doesn't hear them. "Have you not known?
Have you not heard, that the everlasting God, the LORD, the
Creator of the ends of the earth, does not faint, nor is He weary?...
He gives power to the faint, and to those who have no might He
increases strength...but those who wait upon the LORD shall
renew their strength; they shall mount up with wings as eagles,
they shall run and not be weary, and they shall walk and not faint"
(Isa. 40:28–31, MEV).

The word *wait* means "hope for, wait for...look forward with
confidence to that which is good and beneficial."[5] Those who look
with confidence to the Alpha and Omega shall renew their strength
and shall not grow weary. Jesus, who is the Alpha and Omega, is
intimately aware of your every need and struggle. He will fill you
with His strength and carry you in His bosom. Remember, "For
He has said: 'I will never leave you, nor forsake you.' So we may
boldly say: 'The Lord is my helper; I will not fear. What can man
do to me?'" (Heb. 13:5–6, MEV).

Glory be to God and to His Son Jesus, who is the Alpha and
Omega. Let our hearts and minds be filled with the bigness of our
God.

Meditate on these verses:

For it was in Him that all things were created, in heaven
and on earth, things seen and things unseen, whether
thrones, dominions, rulers, or authorities; all things were

created and exist through Him [by His service, intervention] and in and for Him. And He Himself existed before all things, and in Him all things consist (cohere, are held together).

—COLOSSIANS 1:16–17, AMPC

[But] in the last of these days He has spoken to us in [the person of a] Son, Whom He appointed Heir and lawful Owner of all things, also by and through Whom He created the worlds and the reaches of space and the ages of time [He made, produced, built, operated, and arranged them in order]. He is the sole expression of the glory of God [the Light-being, the out-raying or radiance of the divine], and He is the perfect imprint and very image of [God's] nature, upholding and maintaining and guiding and propelling the universe by His mighty word of power.

—HEBREWS 1:2–3, AMPC

The One who loves us is the Alpha and Omega. He is preeminent above all things. He who measures the universe with the span of His hand has you ever before His face.

Prayer

Father, fill my mind with the awesomeness and vastness of who You are. You are before all things; You are the Alpha. You are after all things, the Omega. And You fill everything in between. Help my heart and mind to stay focused on You, Your greatness, and Your utter supremacy in all things. You who measure the universe with the span of Your hand have also numbered the hairs on my head. You who love me know me altogether. I choose to wait on You. In Jesus' holy name, amen.

THE FIRST AND THE LAST

Day 14

I am...the First and the Last.

—REVELATION 1:11

GOD IS THE First and the Last. This designation was ascribed to Jehovah by Isaiah three times (41:4; 44:6; 48:12) and by the apostle John three times in Revelation (1:11; 2:8; 22:13). Richard of St. Victor comments thus: "I am the first and the last. First through creation, last through retribution. First, because before me a God was not formed; last, because after me there shall not be another. First, because all things are from me; last, because all things are to me; from me the beginning, to me the end. First, because I am the cause of origin; last, because I am the judge and the end" (cit. by Trench).[1]

Most of our translations have four occurrences of the phrase "the First and the Last" in Revelation, which includes Revelation 1:11, but some of the oldest manuscripts omit this. We are going to look at these four instances and build upon the revelation laid out in them.

It can almost seem redundant that Jesus says "Alpha and Omega," then "First and the Last," and even later adds "beginning and the end," but He does this for a reason. These three phrases do not mean the same thing. "Alpha and Omega" speaks of divine order and authority, but "First and Last" points us to God being the One who is and was and is to come. Specifically, it points us to the unique role Jesus plays in all of creation and in our redemption.

Revelation 2:8 gives us more insight. "To the angel of the church in Smyrna write: 'The First and the Last, who was dead and came to life'" (MEV). Being fully one with the Father, Jesus shares all the attributes of Jehovah God, but He also had a unique role when He came to this earth and took on the form of a man. I find it instructive to note that Jesus in Revelation 2:8 focused on His death, burial, and resurrection.

For me "the First and the Last" points us to the incarnate Christ. Jesus, being fully God, emptied Himself of all His divine attributes and humbled Himself to become a man just like you and me.

> Who, although being essentially one with God and in the form of God [possessing the fullness of the attributes which make God God], did not think this equality with God was a thing to be eagerly grasped or retained, but stripped Himself [of all privileges and rightful dignity], so as to assume the guise of a servant (slave), in that He became like men and was born a human being.
> —PHILIPPIANS 2:6–7, AMPC

Jesus is first because all things were created through Him, but also He is first because He is the first of this new creation. This new creation is where God, for all eternity, in Jesus, is fully human and divine. This mystery of the gospel is profound.

> For in Him the whole fullness of Deity (the Godhead) continues to dwell in bodily form [giving complete expression of the divine nature].
> —COLOSSIANS 2:9, AMPC

In Jesus the fullness of the Godhead continues to dwell in a human resurrected body. We see this in several other descriptions of Jesus, including Son of Man and firstborn among the dead. Jesus turns to John, who falls to the ground as though one dead because of the magnitude of the revelation, and comforts him with these words:

> Do not be afraid; I am the First and the Last. I am He who lives, and was dead, and behold, I am alive forevermore.
> —REVELATION 1:17–18

Jesus reminded John that He was the same man who walked and talked with John. He was the same One that John ate with, laughed with, and served with. He was the same One who John saw die upon the cross, because John was there. Jesus was the same One who was raised from the dead and ascended to heaven before John's eyes.

Jesus laid out an ever-progressive revelation of Himself to prepare an end-time people to overcome unprecedented adversity. Jesus zeroed in on His humanity and victory over death.

He gives us hope that because He lives, we too shall live.

> A little while longer and the world will see Me no more, but you will see Me. Because I live, you will live also. At that day you will know that I am in My Father, and you in Me, and I in you.
>
> —JOHN 14:19–20

Jesus tells us that after He physically died, we would still see Him. The world would not see Him, but He would give us His Holy Spirit. He then said this about the Holy Spirit: "He will guide you into all truth. For He will not speak on His own authority. But He will speak whatever He hears; and He will tell you things that are to come. He will glorify Me, for He will receive from Me and will declare it to you" (John 16:13–14, MEV).

Jesus is saying, "You will see Me in My new resurrected state. Because I have risen from the dead, you too will also live forever." Jesus was the first to face and conquer death, and He will be the One who defeats death forever.

> But now Christ is risen from the dead, and has become the firstfruits of those who have fallen asleep. For since by man came death, by Man also came the resurrection of the dead. For as in Adam all die, even so in Christ all shall be made alive. But each one in his own order: Christ the firstfruits, afterward, those who are Christ's at His coming. Then comes the end, when He delivers the kingdom to God the Father, when He puts an end to

all rule and all authority and power. For He must reign
till He has put all enemies under His feet. The last enemy
that will be destroyed is death.
—1 CORINTHIANS 15:20–26

Jesus upon His resurrection took the authority of death, hell, and the grave, but as the First and the Last He will, in the future, destroy death forever. After the millennial reign and the white throne judgment seat, Jesus, having defeated every power and authority, will present the earth and all its kingdoms to His Father. At this point the final judgments referred to as the second death will be executed. Satan, his angels, and all the dead whose names were not found written in the Book of Life will be cast into the lake of fire. Then death and hades will be cast into the lake of fire.

Then I saw a great white throne and Him who sat on
it, from whose face the earth and the heaven fled away.
And there was found no place for them. And I saw the
dead, small and great, standing before God, and books
were opened. And another book was opened, which is the
Book of Life. And the dead were judged according to their
works, by the things which were written in the books.
The sea gave up the dead who were in it, and Death and
Hades delivered up the dead who were in them. And
they were judged, each one according to his works. Then
Death and Hades were cast into the lake of fire. This is
the second death. And anyone not found written in the
Book of Life was cast into the lake of fire.
—REVELATION 20:11–15

As John saw this revelation of Jesus in all His glory and yet still fully human, he must have been so comforted. John, who was banished on the Isle of Patmos having suffered much, was now seeing Jesus as fully God and fully man saying, "I am the First and I am the Last. I am the First to conquer death, and I am the Last who will ultimately destroy death forever." John's mind might have been filled with this verse from Isaiah:

He will swallow up death [in victory; He will abolish death forever]. And the Lord God will wipe away tears from all faces; and the reproach of His people He will take away from off all the earth; for the Lord has spoken it.

—ISAIAH 25:8, AMPC

Jesus was the First of all humankind to live a sinless life and defeat death. He will be the Last, having overcome the reign of death and put an end to the grave forever. As we focus on Jesus as the First and the Last, let us rejoice in that death is once and forever defeated in Him. He will continue to move forward in His plans and purposes in and through our lives until He vanquishes all powers, authorities, and rulers, and finally judges all who have ever lived. He will cast the wicked into the lake of fire along with death and hades, defeating forever everything that hinders His love. There shall never again, for all of eternity, be any death, for Jesus is the *Last*.

Prayer

Father, thank You that Jesus, as the First and the Last, has conquered death forever. Because Jesus lived a sinless life, bore my punishment through His death, and defeated death when You raised Him from the dead, I too can rest in assurance of my eternal life. All things were created by Him, for Him, and through Him. Jesus will have the last word on all things. I rest in this hope. In Jesus' name, amen.

Day 15
THE SEVEN GOLDEN LAMPSTANDS

Then I turned to see the voice that spoke with me. And having turned I saw seven golden lampstands, and in the midst of the seven lampstands One like the Son of Man.
—REVELATION 1:12-13

JOHN WAS A prisoner on the Isle of Patmos. He was most likely required to work the mines and experienced continual brutal life conditions. There are various theories as to the conditions on Patmos, but the reality is that for many years John lived among other prisoners who had been exiled, and he was cut off from the outside world. John was in the Spirit on the Lord's Day when he had this incredible experience.

The apostle John wrote in Revelation 1:12–17:

> Then I turned to see the voice that spoke with me. And having turned I saw seven golden lampstands, and in the midst of the seven lampstands One like the Son of Man, clothed with a garment down to the feet and girded about the chest with a golden band. His head and hair were white like wool, as white as snow, and His eyes like a flame of fire; His feet were like fine brass, as if refined in a furnace, and His voice as the sound of many waters; He had in His right hand seven stars, out of His mouth went a sharp two-edged sword, and His countenance was like the sun shining in its strength. And when I saw Him, I fell at His feet as dead.

John was the disciple who arguably was closest to Jesus while Jesus was on the earth. He is called John the beloved and was the one who rested his head on Jesus' breast. John was one of the main leaders of the early church, which meant that he was not only an

103

apostle, but he often worked with Peter among the Mediterranean Christians as described in the Book of Acts.

When John heard a voice speaking to him, as he wrote about in Revelation 1:12, he turned around, and the first thing he saw was Jesus in all His glory and might, standing in the midst of seven golden lampstands. This is different from the single candlestick in the Jewish temple, which was one stand with seven candles on branches. This vision showed seven separate lampstands. As stated in *Commentary Critical and Explanatory on the Whole Bible*:

> Here the seven are *separate* candlesticks, typifying, as
> that *one*, the entire Church, but now no longer as the
> Jewish Church (represented by the *one* sevenfold candle-
> stick) restricted to one outward unity and one place; the
> several churches are mutually independent as to external
> ceremonies and government…yet one in the unity of the
> Spirit and the Headship of Christ. The candlestick is not
> light, but the bearer of light, holding it forth to give light
> around. The light is the Lord's, not the Church's; from
> Him she receives it. She is to be a light-bearer to His
> glory.[1]

Here Jesus revealed that He alone was the head of the church and the source of its life and light. John must have been comforted knowing that although he was separated from the churches, Jesus was standing in the midst as the source and unifier of the entire body of Christ.

The local church is Jesus' creation, not man's. The church is the local gathering of believers that Christ dwells in, who come together to reflect His glory and majesty to a lost and dying world.

The true church is built upon the revelation of Jesus. "He said to them, 'But who do you say that I am?' Simon Peter replied, 'You are the Christ, the Son of the living God.' Jesus answered him, 'Blessed are you, Simon son of Jonah, for flesh and blood has not revealed this to you, but My Father who is in heaven'" (Matt. 16:15–17, MEV).

Then Jesus introduced His eternal plan to exercise and establish

His kingdom upon the earth. Jesus declared that He was going to build His church.

> And I also say to you that you are Peter, and on this rock
> I will build My church, and the gates of Hades shall not
> prevail against it.
>
> —MATTHEW 16:18

This declaration is even more profound when you realize that Jesus was at Caesarea Philippi. This town was located at the base of Mount Hermon. A large spring was located very near a huge rock structure where there was an ancient temple to the Greek god Pan. This city was kind of the red-light district of northern Galilee. The people believed that out of the caves where the water flowed was the entrance to the underworld—literally the gates of hell. They worshipped Pan, a god of fertility but also a god associated with panic, fear, and night terrors. "In order to entice the return of their god, Pan, each year, the people of Caesarea Philippi engaged in horrible deeds, including prostitution and sexual interaction between humans and goats."[2]

Jesus announced at this ungodly location that He was going to defeat all the powers of darkness and establish His kingdom on the earth by building a church through the revelation of who He really is. During this amazing moment, Jesus laid the foundation for the establishment of His church and the authority and power the church would exercise in the earth.

> I will give you the keys of the kingdom of heaven; and
> whatever you bind (declare to be improper and unlawful)
> on earth must be what is already bound in heaven; and
> whatever you loose (declare lawful) on earth must be
> what is already loosed in heaven.
>
> —MATTHEW 16:19, AMPC

This Amplified Bible, Classic Edition describes the correct context and function of the church's authority. We don't just randomly bind and loose things according to whatever we want. We, by revelation, behold what is going on in heaven, and then we have the authority to declare and release heaven's ways into the earth. When we read that Jesus stood in the midst of the seven lampstands, we remember that we are His church. We are here to reveal Him and exercise His authority and kingdom on the earth.

Unfortunately, in so many places today the "churches" conform to the gates of hell and don't overcome them. We allow the world and its culture to dictate to us what truth is. We compromise, hoping to win the approval of man at the expense of alienating Jesus. (Just read the rebukes of God's churches in Revelation chapters 2 and 3.)

The apostle Paul wrote, "[For I always pray to] the God of our Lord Jesus Christ, the Father of glory, that He may grant you a spirit of wisdom and revelation [of insight into mysteries and secrets] in the [deep and intimate] knowledge of Him" (Eph. 1:17, AMPC). Paul was praying by the power of the Holy Spirit that we would be filled with the revelation knowledge of who Jesus is. This intimate, personal, ever-growing revelation will empower us to understand the plan and purpose of God in and through our lives.

> By having the eyes of your heart flooded with light, so that you can know and understand the hope to which He has called you, and how rich is His glorious inheritance in the saints (His set-apart ones), and [so that you can know and understand] what is the immeasurable and unlimited and surpassing greatness of His power in and for us who believe, as demonstrated in the working of His mighty strength.
>
> —EPHESIANS 1:18–19, AMPC

The ability to exercise the power and authority of the kingdom is directly connected to the depth of our deep personal and intimate revelation knowledge of Him.

> Which He exerted in Christ when He raised Him from the dead and seated Him at His [own] right hand in the heavenly [places].
>
> —EPHESIANS 1:20, AMPC

Now Paul establishes the authority and power of Jesus in direct connection to the church.

> Far above all rule and authority and power and dominion and every name that is named [above every title that can be conferred], not only in this age and in this world, but also in the age and the world which are to come. And He has put all things under His feet and has appointed Him the universal and supreme Head of the church [a headship exercised throughout the church], which is His body, the fullness of Him Who fills all in all [for in that body lives the full measure of Him Who makes everything complete, and Who fills everything everywhere with Himself].
> —EPHESIANS 1:21–23, AMPC; SEE ALSO PSALM 8:6

The church is the vehicle through which the fullness of God is to be released into the earth. When you see Jesus standing in the midst of the seven lampstands, know that His kingdom plans and purposes will be done in the earth through His church. God will reveal the fullness of Himself to all humanity, even the principalities and powers, through the church.

> And to make all see what is the fellowship of the mystery, which from the beginning of the ages has been hidden in God who created all things through Jesus Christ; to the intent that now the manifold wisdom of God might be made known by the church to the principalities and powers in the heavenly places, according to the eternal purpose which He accomplished in Christ Jesus our Lord, in whom we have boldness and access with confidence through faith in Him. Therefore I ask that you do not lose heart at my tribulations for you, which is your glory.
> —EPHESIANS 3:9–13

Paul says do not lose heart. The fullness of who God is and His plan for the end of the age and eternity is going to manifest and be revealed through the church. The greatest of all love stories will be fulfilled through the church.

Do not allow the devil to cause you to be separated from God's collective body, the church. We together are the vehicle through which Jesus is going to fulfill His end-time purpose. Are there problems? Yes; but there were problems in John's day. (See Revelation 2–3.) But Jesus is going to cleanse, purify, rebuke, encourage, and perfect His church to be His glorious bride.

> Christ also loved the church and gave Himself for her, that He might sanctify and cleanse her with the washing of water by the word, that He might present her to Himself a glorious church, not having spot or wrinkle or any such thing, but that she should be holy and without blemish.
> —EPHESIANS 5:25–27

Prayer

Father, the church is Your vehicle through which Jesus' plans and purposes will be fulfilled and Your glory released in the earth. Let me rightly relate to Your church and find my place in it. Help me not to separate or isolate myself from Your body, the church, but to love it as Jesus also loves it. Jesus, You said, "I will build My church, and the gates of Hades shall not prevail against it" (Matt. 16:18). Build Your church with me as a member, for Your plans and Your purposes. In Jesus' name, amen.

Day 16

THE SON OF MAN, PART 1

Then I turned to see the voice that spoke with me. And having turned I saw seven golden lampstands, and in the midst of the seven lampstands One like the Son of Man.
—REVELATION 1:12–13

JESUS USED THE title "Son of Man" eighty-five times in Scripture, but He used the title "Son of God" only seven times.

This is interesting because the phrase "Son of Man" was used in the Old Testament mainly to denote the weakness and fragility of man. Ezekiel invoked the title the most. Only after Ezekiel's prophetic writings during the Babylonian captivity did Daniel several decades later use the phrase to describe the coming Messiah.

The revelation of Jesus as the Son of Man is probably the most significant of all the titles given to Jesus. The truth of Jesus as a man is at the core of the gospel message and the redemption story. We will take the next three days to explore this amazing truth.

The fact that Jesus came in human flesh is astounding when you think about it. God, who has always existed, left His position of divinity and limited Himself into the body of a man. Jesus didn't just take on human form; He emptied Himself of all His divine attributes and became fully human.

> Let this same attitude and purpose and [humble] mind be in you which was in Christ Jesus: [Let Him be your example in humility:] Who, although being essentially one with God and in the form of God [possessing the fullness of the attributes which make God God], did not think this equality with God was a thing to be eagerly grasped or retained, but stripped Himself [of all privileges and rightful dignity], so as to assume the guise of a servant (slave), in that He became like men and was born a human being.
> —PHILIPPIANS 2:5–7, AMPC

The three main aspects of God are omniscience, omnipresence, and omnipotence. Omniscience is that God is all-knowing. Jesus was not all-knowing on the earth. "And Jesus increased in wisdom (in broad and full understanding) and in stature and years, and in favor with God and man" (Luke 2:52, AMPC). "But of that day and hour no one knows, not even the angels in heaven, nor the Son, but only the Father" (Mark 13:32). Jesus clearly did not have all knowledge while on the earth.

Omnipresence means being present everywhere. Jesus was limited to the human body He was in. He felt the same things we feel emotionally and physically. Jesus left His omnipresence to take on human form.

Omnipotence means that God is all-powerful, but Jesus repeatedly stated that He could do nothing of Himself. He emptied Himself of His divine power. "Jesus said to him, 'Have I been with you such a long time, and yet you have not known Me, Philip? He who has seen Me has seen the Father. So how can you say, "Show us the Father"? Do you not believe that I am in the Father and the Father is in Me? The words that I say to you I do not speak on My own authority. But the Father who lives in Me does the works'" (John 14:9–10, MEV).

This emptying of Himself is called the kenosis. It is the doctrine that Jesus emptied Himself of the divinity that He had in heaven. Jesus did not cease being divine. He set aside His divinity and took on the form of humanity. All of His miracles, His preaching, and His total obedience to the Father were done through the power of God given by the Holy Spirit.

It is extremely important to understand that Jesus lived a human life, albeit free from a sin nature, but in all ways subject to the same weaknesses, temptations, stresses, and vulnerabilities that we face. "For we do not have a High Priest who cannot sympathize with our weaknesses, but One who was in every sense tempted like we are, yet without sin" (Heb. 4:15, MEV).

Jesus has always been God, but when He came to the earth and humbled Himself, He took on the form of Son of Man.

> In the beginning was the Word, and the Word was with
> God, and the Word was God. He was in the beginning
> with God. All things were made through Him, and
> without Him nothing was made that was made....And
> the Word became flesh and dwelt among us, and we
> beheld His glory, the glory as of the only begotten of the
> Father, full of grace and truth.
>
> —JOHN 1:1–3, 14

Jesus had to come as a man, live as a man, and die as a man.
God gave dominion to man. "Then God said, 'Let us make man
in our image, after our likeness, and let them have dominion over
the fish of the sea, and over the birds of the air, and over the livestock, and over all the earth, and over every creeping thing that
creeps on the earth'" (Gen. 1:26, MEV).

Man rejected God's authority and sinned. God declared, "The
wages of sin is death" (Rom. 6:23). "Therefore, just as through one
man [Adam] sin entered the world, and death through sin, and
thus death spread to all men, because all sinned" (Rom. 5:12).

Since man is the one who sinned, only a man could pay the
price for sin, which was death. God declared that sin entered
because of one man's disobedience, and his sin made us all guilty;
therefore, one sinless man could also pay the price as a substitute
for the guilty.

> Therefore, as through one man's offense judgment came
> to all men, resulting in condemnation, even so through
> one Man's righteous act the free gift came to all men,
> resulting in justification of life. For as by one man's dis-
> obedience many were made sinners, so also by one Man's
> obedience many will be made righteous.
>
> —ROMANS 5:18–19

Jesus could only represent man and pay the price for man if He
was a man. He also could only be an acceptable substitute if He
was truly innocent. Only an innocent man could pay the price for

the guilty. It was necessary for Jesus to come as fully man and live a sinless life to qualify as an acceptable substitute.

In the Old Testament, God required sacrificial lambs to be spotless and without defect. They represented the need for an innocent and pure substitute for the guilty. The lambs and other sacrifices were only a temporary substitute until the time that Jesus, the Son of Man, would come to earth, live a sinless life, and pay the price for our judgment.

Only a man could pay the price and take back dominion. When man yielded to Satan in the Garden of Eden, he released death into God's creation. From that moment on, everything under man's dominion would suffer the consequences of sin.

Romans 8:18–23 tells us that creation was subject to decay and destruction because man sinned, and he had dominion over the earth. Man, through his disobedience to God, released the kingdom of darkness into the earth. Only man can release the kingdom rulership of God back into the earth. All of creation waits for the manifestation of the sons of God. Because all have sinned and fallen short of the glory of God, only Jesus as the Son of Man could reconcile and restore what was lost through man's disobedience.

When we see Jesus as the Son of Man, we understand that He feels our weaknesses because He had those weaknesses when He was a man. He understands our temptations because He too was tempted in all points as we are. He helps us through our struggles because He too had to lean on His Father through the Holy Spirit to overcome sin.

The idea that Jesus came to this earth and took on humanity is one of the great mysteries of the depth of His love. He gave up more than we could ever know to become human, but it did not stop there.

> But made Himself of no reputation, taking the form
> of a bondservant, and coming in the likeness of men.
> And being found in appearance as a man, He humbled

> Himself and became obedient to the point of death, even the death of the cross.
>
> —PHILIPPIANS 2:7–8

Jesus, being fully God, allowed Himself to suffer. He suffered temptation, He suffered rejection, He suffered betrayal, He suffered being lied about, and He suffered being stolen from.

> For consider Him who endured such hostility from sinners against Himself, lest you become weary and discouraged in your souls. You have not yet resisted to bloodshed, striving against sin.
>
> —HEBREWS 12:3–4

Jesus was tortured, beaten, spat upon, plotted against, whipped, punched, scorned, and ultimately crucified. When we see God becoming fully the Son of Man and allowing Himself to be treated so horribly, it gives us strength to endure our sufferings. When we consider Him suffering as a man, it empowers us to not grow weary and discouraged in our souls.

One of the strategies of Satan is to get us to dwell on our suffering and the injustices we have endured. This opens the door for us to become bitter, resentful, vengeful, and full of unforgiveness. Jesus, the innocent Son of God, became the Son of Man to redeem us. We did not deserve this. We cannot ever repay Him. The truth is that we all deserve death, but Jesus gave us life. "For all have sinned and fall short of the glory of God" (Rom. 3:23).

> As it is written: "There is none righteous, no, not one; there is none who understands; there is none who seeks after God. They have all turned aside; they have together become unprofitable; there is none who does good, no, not one.
>
> "Their throat is an open tomb; with their tongues they have practiced deceit;
>
> "The poison of asps is under their lips;
>
> "Whose mouth is full of cursing and bitterness.

"Their feet are swift to shed blood; destruction and misery are in their ways; and the way of peace they have not known.

"There is no fear of God before their eyes."

—ROMANS 3:10–18

We tend to see Jesus as the innocent Son of Man, but we must also recognize that we, in this life, may suffer because of our own sins and the sins of humanity. Jesus was the only innocent one who truly did not deserve anything He suffered. Some may think this is harsh, but I like to tell people, "The only thing I deserve is an eternity in hell." This is the truth. We all deserve hell. Thanks be to God for sending Jesus as the Son of Man to suffer for us so that we may live for and with Him forever.

Prayer

Father, thank You for sending Your Son Jesus as the Son of Man. Jesus, You emptied Yourself of all Your divine attributes and suffered as man. You are able to relate to all my weaknesses and temptations because You too had to endure being tempted in all points as I am. Because You overcame the world, I can have courage that I too, through Your strength, can stand strong in the midst of suffering. Fill me with Your patient endurance today. In Jesus' holy name, amen.

Day 17
THE SON OF MAN, PART 2

For the Son of Man has come to save that which was lost.
—Matthew 18:11

WHEN JESUS CALLED Himself the Son of Man, He was identifying with humanity.

- Jesus is saying, "I am one of you forever." He will be fully God and fully man forever. Daniel used the Son of Man title to speak of God's eternal destiny as a man on the earth. This truth is vital for us to understand who Jesus is and what He is doing in the days we are living in.

- Jesus embraced the frailty of humanity during His time on earth. The phrase *son of man* was used in the Old Testament to refer to weak humans. Ezekiel used this term nearly a hundred times to emphasize his own human frailty in being a weak man made of clay. It is incredible to think that God became a human, a son of man, and was hungry, tired, thirsty, and needy, just like all men are.

- Jesus is committed to walking in complete unity with us. He fully shares all that He is and all that He has with those who are redeemed. His eternal companions are human. He will bring His bride into the glory that He inherits as a man from the Father. When the Bible says in Romans 8:19 that "the earnest expectation of the creation eagerly waits for the revealing of the sons of God," it is talking about when we will be like Him, fully human yet one flesh with Jesus.

In the previous chapter we looked at Jesus as a man in weakness and yet in the full strength of the Holy Spirit. Today we will see the power of Jesus on this earth as the Son of Man. Jesus sent us into the world just as the Father sent Him. "So Jesus said to them again, 'Peace to you! As the Father has sent Me, I also send you'" (John 20:21).

Jesus unveiled this incredible truth during His earthly ministry. He showed that God's power and authority are eternally invested in those who are redeemed through Christ Jesus.

1. Jesus, as the Son of Man, has life in Himself and the authority to execute judgment.

> For as the Father has life in Himself, so He has granted the Son to have life in Himself, and has given Him authority to execute judgment also, because He is the Son of Man.
> —JOHN 5:26–27

The Father granted authority to Jesus to execute judgment because He is the Son of Man. Dominion had been given to humanity. Man used his authority to release the kingdom of darkness into the world, and thus death. Jesus came to redeem humanity, pay the price for man's disobedience, and fully re-establish the authority of the kingdom of God in the created realm. God gave authority and dominion to man. Jesus as the Son of Man reclaimed man's role as God's delegated authority to establish the kingdom of heaven's rulership in the earth. Just like Jesus, we too shall judge in the age to come.

> Do you not know that the saints will judge the world?...
> Do you not know that we shall judge angels?
> —1 CORINTHIANS 6:2–3

Jesus, being firstborn from the dead, reveals our eternal authority through the title Son of Man.

2. Jesus, as the Son of Man, has power to forgive.

"But that you may know that the Son of Man has power on earth to forgive sins"—He said to the man who was paralyzed, "I say to you, arise, take up your bed, and go to your house."

—LUKE 5:24

Jesus declared that as the Son of Man, He had authority to forgive sins. Jesus then told the disciples after the resurrection that they too could forgive sins. "If you forgive the sins of any, they are forgiven them; if you retain the sins of any, they are retained" (John 20:23). This is a great mystery that has led to much confusion in its application, but Jesus said it, and it fits with everything He said about Himself as the Son of Man and about our partnership with Him.

3. Jesus, as the Son of Man, is Lord of the harvest. He sows the seed and will reap the harvest.

He answered and said to them: "He who sows the good seed is the Son of Man. The field is the world, the good seeds are the sons of the kingdom, but the tares are the sons of the wicked one. The enemy who sowed them is the devil, the harvest is the end of the age, and the reapers are the angels. Therefore as the tares are gathered and burned in the fire, so it will be at the end of this age. The Son of Man will send out His angels, and they will gather out of His kingdom all things that offend, and those who practice lawlessness, and will cast them into the furnace of fire. There will be wailing and gnashing of teeth. Then the righteous will shine forth as the sun in the kingdom of their Father. He who has ears to hear, let him hear!"

—MATTHEW 13:37–43

While on the earth, Jesus as the Son of Man sowed His people as good seed into the earth. Jesus taught, "You are the light of the world....Let your light so shine before men that they may see your good works and glorify your Father who is in heaven" (Matt. 5:14–16, MEV).

Jesus also said in Matthew 13 that He, as the Son of Man, at the end of the age will have authority to send out the angels to gather the harvest. The Son of Man will remove everything on this earth that offends. In other words, everything that is opposed to God and hinders His kingdom rulership will be cast into the fire.

4. Jesus, as the Son of Man, was given power to reconcile the lost to the Father.

> For the Son of Man has come to save that which was lost.
> —MATTHEW 18:11

We too have now been commissioned to bring the gospel to reconcile men to God. "Now all things are of God, who has reconciled us to Himself through Jesus Christ, and has given us the ministry of reconciliation, that is, that God was in Christ reconciling the world to Himself...and has committed to us the word of reconciliation. Now then, we are ambassadors for Christ, as though God were pleading through us: we implore you on Christ's behalf, be reconciled to God" (2 Cor. 5:18–20).

5. Jesus, as the Son of Man, revealed how power and authority are exercised.

> You know that the rulers of the Gentiles lord it over them, and those who are great exercise authority over them. Yet it shall not be so among you; but whoever desires to become great among you, let him be your servant. And whoever desires to be first among you, let him be your slave—just as the Son of Man did not come to be served, but to serve, and to give His life a ransom for many.
> —MATTHEW 20:25–28

Jesus as the Son of Man laid down His life for many. We too are commissioned by Jesus to lay down our lives for others. "If anyone will come after Me, let him deny himself, and take up his cross, and follow Me. For whoever would save his life will lose it, and whoever loses his life for My sake will find it" (Matt. 16:24–25, MEV).

6. Jesus was resurrected as the Son of Man.

> Now as they came down from the mountain, He commanded them that they should tell no one the things they had seen, till the Son of Man had risen from the dead. So they kept this word to themselves, questioning what the rising from the dead meant.
>
> —MARK 9:9–10

We too will be resurrected. "For the Lord Himself will descend from heaven with a shout, with the voice of the archangel, and with the trumpet of God. And the dead in Christ will rise first. Then we who are alive and remain shall be caught up together with them in the clouds to meet the Lord in the air. And so we shall be forever with the Lord. Therefore comfort one another with these words" (1 Thess. 4:16–18, MEV).

7. Jesus was betrayed as the Son of Man.

> But behold, the hand of My betrayer is with Me on the table. And truly the Son of Man goes as it has been determined, but woe to that man by whom He is betrayed!
>
> —LUKE 22:21–22

We also can expect to be betrayed. "Then they will hand you over to be persecuted and will kill you. And you will be hated by all nations for My name's sake. Then many will fall away, and betray one another, and hate one another" (Matt. 24:9–10, MEV).

8. Jesus, as the Son of Man, was a prophetic sign to His generation. His death, burial, and resurrection prove that He is from the Father.

> For as Jonah became a sign to the Ninevites, so also the Son of Man will be to this generation.
>
> —LUKE 11:30

We also are a prophetic sign to our generation. "Only let your conduct be worthy of the gospel of Christ…that you stand fast in one spirit, with one mind striving together for the faith of the gospel, and not in any way terrified by your adversaries, which is to them a proof of perdition, but to you of salvation, and that from God. For to you it has been granted on behalf of Christ, not only to believe in Him, but also to suffer for His sake" (Phil. 1:27–29).

9. Angels ministered to Jesus as the Son of Man.

> Most assuredly, I say to you, hereafter you shall see heaven open, and the angels of God ascending and descending upon the Son of Man.
>
> —JOHN 1:51

> Then the devil left Him, and behold, angels came and ministered to Him.
>
> —MATTHEW 4:11

> Then an angel appeared to Him from heaven, strengthening Him.
>
> —LUKE 22:43

God has also declared that we too shall have angels minister to us and strengthen us. "Are they not all ministering spirits sent out to minister to those who will inherit salvation?" (Heb. 1:14, MEV). "For He shall give His angels charge over you to guard you in all your ways. They shall bear you up in their hands, lest you strike your foot against a stone" (Ps. 91:11–12, MEV).

10. Jesus, as the Son of Man, through the Holy Spirit was able to access heaven even while He lived in a human body on the earth. John 3:13 says, "No one has ascended to heaven but He who came down from heaven, that is, the Son of Man who is in heaven." He didn't say the Son of Man who was in heaven or who will be in heaven, but the Son of Man who *is* in heaven. This is a great and powerful truth and mystery. Jesus was fully man, yet He was also perfectly connected to the Father and the heavenly realm by the Holy Spirit.

Jesus, like Adam before the fall, walked in two realms at the same time: the natural realm and the heavenly realm. The Garden of Eden was in both realms. God walked in the garden. The Scripture never implies that God the Father became incarnate or took on human form to fellowship with Adam. Adam and the garden existed in a dual realm of natural and spiritual.

When God drove Adam and Eve from the garden, He used cherubim, angelic beings, to guard and block access to the garden and the tree of life. "So He drove out the man; and He placed cherubim at the east of the garden of Eden, and a flaming sword which turned every way, to guard the way to the tree of life" (Gen. 3:24). In essence, the Garden of Eden was foreshadowing God's plan that we would dwell in heaven near the throne of God.

> And he showed me a pure river of water of life, clear as crystal, proceeding from the throne of God and of the Lamb. In the middle of its street, and on either side of the river, was the tree of life....And there shall be no more curse, but the throne of God and of the Lamb shall be in it....They shall see His face, and His name shall be on their foreheads....And they shall reign forever and ever.
> —Revelation 22:1–5

The tree of life in the new Jerusalem will also be in a dual realm of heavenly and natural. Jesus as a sinless man walked in this dual realm. Sin is what caused man to no longer be able to walk in both realms. Jesus restored us to walk in both realms, at least in part. I say in part because although I believe it is accessible, I have yet to meet anyone who has completely obtained this level. But as we get closer to the return of Christ, we will experience more of living in both realms at the same time. The promises of God and His calling for us to live in His heavenly realm are clear.

Paul declares that God "raised us up together, and made us sit together in the heavenly places in Christ Jesus" (Eph. 2:6). The wall between the natural and spirit realms is coming down. As we grow in the revelation of Jesus as the Son of Man, we will walk more like Him on this earth.

11. Jesus, as the Son of Man, revealed that the human frame would be the eternal dwelling place of the fullness of God.

> For in Him the whole fullness of Deity (the Godhead) continues to dwell in bodily form [giving complete expression of the divine nature].
>
> —COLOSSIANS 2:9, AMPC

In Jesus as the Son of Man, God merged the heavenly and the natural realms for all eternity. The human frame is the chosen dwelling place of God for eternity. Jesus created "in Himself one new man from the two, thus making peace, and that He might reconcile them both to God in one body through the cross, thereby putting to death the enmity" (Eph. 2:15–16).

12. The revelation of Jesus as the Son of Man causes us to want to live holy and pure lives. When we see Jesus as the Son of Man and know that we too shall have resurrected bodies, we look at ourselves differently. We do not want to do anything to pollute or violate our bodies because we know that they are God's holy temples. We want to walk just as He walks. This understanding—that your body is His temple—is the greatest motivation to live a pure life.

> Flee sexual immorality. Every sin that a man does is outside the body, but he who commits sexual immorality sins against his own body. Or do you not know that your body is the temple of the Holy Spirit who is in you, whom you have from God, and you are not your own? For you were bought at a price; therefore glorify God in your body and in your spirit, which are God's.
>
> —1 CORINTHIANS 6:18–20

> Therefore [with the revelation of Jesus as the Son of Man] gird up the loins of your mind, be sober, and rest your hope fully upon the grace that is to be brought to you at the revelation of Jesus Christ; as obedient children, not conforming yourselves to the former lusts, as in your

ignorance; but as He who called you is holy, you also be holy in all your conduct, because it is written, "Be holy, for I am holy."

—1 PETER 1:13–16

Prayer

Father, fill me with the understanding of the power, authority, privilege, and responsibility of being a son of man. As I see Jesus, I also see what You have called me to be. Establish Your kingdom authority in and through me in my areas of influence. Cause me to desire to be that holy temple and Your eternal dwelling place. As You have sent Jesus, even so You send me. I yield to Your will. In Jesus' holy name, amen.

Day 18
THE ONE WHO WILL RULE AND REIGN FOREVER

Yet I have set My King on My holy hill of Zion. I will declare the decree: The LORD has said to Me, "You are My Son, today I have begotten You. Ask of Me, and I will give You the nations for Your inheritance, and the ends of the earth for Your possession."

—PSALM 2:6-8

JESUS, AS THE Son of Man, will rule and reign forever. We have looked for two days at Jesus as the Son of Man, and we are now going to enter the most powerful part: the coming of Jesus as the Son of Man. The end of the age, the climax of the ages, and the grand event we are all waiting for is the second coming of Christ.

As John wrote about this vision, his thoughts of the prophet Daniel must have been at the forefront of his mind. The revelation of Jesus as the Son of Man will cause the most dramatic shift of understanding concerning the coming of the end of the age. Jesus, as a man, is coming back to the earth to rule and reign. This one new man, the God/Man, the resurrected Christ, who for all of eternity will retain His human body and yet still be fully God, filled and flooded with the Godhead, is the great mystery of all time.

This understanding is also key to discerning the time in which we will see this reality manifested. Let's look at the events of Daniel's prophecy. Daniel has a vision of the four great world kingdoms as well as the rise of the Antichrist and the Antichrist's kingdom.

> After this I saw in the night visions, and behold, a fourth beast, dreadful and terrible, exceedingly strong. It had huge iron teeth; it was devouring, breaking in pieces, and trampling the residue with its feet. It was different from

all the beasts that were before it, and it had ten horns. I was considering the horns, and there was another horn, a little one, coming up among them, before whom three of the first horns were plucked out by the roots. And there, in this horn, were eyes like the eyes of a man, and a mouth speaking pompous words.

—DANIEL 7:7–8

Daniel was deeply troubled by what he saw and asked an angel standing by him to explain it. He especially wanted to know about this fourth, most terrible beast. The angel said:

The fourth beast shall be a fourth kingdom on earth, which shall be different from all other kingdoms, and shall devour the whole earth, trample it and break it in pieces. The ten horns are ten kings who shall arise from this kingdom. And another shall rise after them; he shall be different from the first ones, and shall subdue three kings. He shall speak pompous words against the Most High, shall persecute the saints of the Most High, and shall intend to change times and law. Then the saints shall be given into his hand for a time and times and half a time.

—DANIEL 7:23–25

This prophecy is speaking of the great tribulation and the Antichrist's war against God and His people. But in the middle of the vision an amazing thing takes place. God the Father, called the Ancient of Days, sets up a court in the heavenlies to oversee the end of the age and execute judgment upon the Antichrist's kingdom.

I watched till thrones were put in place, and the Ancient of Days was seated; His garment was white as snow, and the hair of His head was like pure wool. His throne was a fiery flame, its wheels a burning fire; a fiery stream issued and came forth from before Him. A thousand thousands ministered to Him; ten thousand times ten

thousand stood before Him. The court was seated, and
the books were opened.

—DANIEL 7:9–10

The Father is seated in the court of heaven among several thrones, and then the court is seated. The members of the
court very likely are the twenty-four elders of Revelation. When
everyone is seated, the books are opened. "And I saw the dead,
small and great, standing before God. Books were opened. Then
another book was opened, which is the Book of Life" (Rev. 20:12,
MEV). The books are believed to record the deeds of men, and the
Book of Life contains the names of those who are born again.

This was an amazing sight for Daniel! First he saw God the
Father in all His glory, then he saw the court of heaven, and then
a man came into the scene. Imagine what flooded Daniel's mind
when he saw a man riding on the clouds of heaven and coming
into the presence of almighty God.

I was watching in the night visions, and behold, One like
the Son of Man, coming with the clouds of heaven! He
came to the Ancient of Days, and they brought Him near
before Him.

—DANIEL 7:13

What man can ride on the clouds of heaven? What man can
be brought right up to the throne of almighty God? This scene is
overwhelming. Who is this man? "One like the Son of Man."

Then a most incredible thing happened. God the Father handed
over His authority to this man to rule and reign forever.

Then to Him was given dominion and glory and a
kingdom, that all peoples, nations, and languages should
serve Him. His dominion is an everlasting dominion,
which shall not pass away, and His kingdom the one
which shall not be destroyed.

—DANIEL 7:14

The Son of Man in this vision, as we now know, is Jesus in His resurrected human body. The idea that a man could come to the Ancient of Days, riding on the clouds of heaven, and be given all power, glory, authority, and an eternal kingdom was revolutionary in Daniel's day. This man would never die, and His dominion was everlasting.

Many years later, the apostle John saw Jesus as this same Son of Man standing in the midst of the seven golden lampstands. The sight was too much for John, and he fell to the ground as though dead.

Jesus is coming back to the earth as a man, yet fully God, to rule and reign here. However, He will not reign alone. "But the saints of the Most High shall take the kingdom and possess the kingdom forever, even forever and ever" (Dan. 7:18, MEV). We too shall reign with Christ, and we too shall receive this kingdom from God the Father through Jesus.

A season is coming when the Antichrist will gain global power— not complete control, but more power than any king before him. He will be more terrible than any before him and will make war against God and His people. Not everyone will serve the Antichrist. There will be many who resist him, not just the tribulation saints. I agree with various scholars that the Antichrist's control will not be absolute but so extensive that the Scripture refers to it allegorically as the whole world.

Satan's focus will be an anti (opposite, instead of, substitution)[1] for the real Christ. Jesus, being one with God and having taken on the form of man, dying for our sins, raised from the dead, and returning as a resurrected man, will be the antithesis of what the Antichrist will project. Satan's kingdom and message will be the exaltation of man as his own god. The worship of the Antichrist will be more the worship of *mankind* than of a singular man. He will offer the lie that man, without God, can rule and reign, and maybe even have a form of eternal life.

We do not yet know what this will look like, but the image of the beast that speaks points us in this direction. "He was granted power to give breath to the image of the beast, that the image of

the beast should both speak and cause as many as would not worship the image of the beast to be killed" (Rev. 13:15). This creation
will have life and an intelligent conscience. Until recently this
would seem impossible, but with the push for transhumanism and
advances in genetic engineering, it's easy to see that maybe the
Antichrist will present a form of "eternal life" and the evolution of
humans into their own godlike beings.

There clearly will be a supernatural element to the image of
the beast. It will be "according to the working of Satan, with all
power, signs, and lying wonders, and with all unrighteous deception among those who perish" (2 Thess. 2:9–10). These supernatural manifestations will convince people that they need no
religion, they do not need a savior, and they do not need God. The
beast will convince many that Christianity is an enemy of the new
reality he is presenting and they, the Christians, are stopping the
rise of a new world order of a new humanity.

Jesus will return as the true God who joins Himself with us
for eternity. The Antichrist will present himself as a substitution,
someone to believe instead of Christ. He will fool people into
believing that they have obtained their own godlikeness. We don't
know exactly how this will manifest, but understanding Jesus as
the Son of Man is vital to understanding Satan's end-time plan
because Satan, through the Antichrist, will offer a substitution for
Jesus Christ.

Is it possible that the Antichrist will present a way that seems to
have removed the fear of death and thus supposedly removed the
need for Jesus? Could this be why he "shall speak pompous words
against the Most High" (Dan. 7:25)?

There will be a massive spirit of deception. God will turn
people over to believe these lies. "The coming of the lawless one
is according to the working of Satan, with all power, signs, and
lying wonders, and with all unrighteous deception among those
who perish, because they did not receive the love of the truth, that
they might be saved. And for this reason God will send them
strong delusion, that they should believe the lie, that they all may

be condemned who did not believe the truth but had pleasure in unrighteousness" (2 Thess. 2:9–12).

Even though we see through a glass darkly and can only speculate on the coming events, we know the beast will be given power for a short season. "Then he opened his mouth in blasphemy against God, to blaspheme His name, His tabernacle, and those who dwell in heaven" (Rev. 13:6).

The kings of the earth in union with the beast will attempt to remove all influence of God

> The kings of the earth set themselves, and the rulers take counsel together, against the LORD and against His Anointed, saying, "Let us break Their bonds in pieces and cast away Their cords from us."
>
> —PSALM 2:2–3

God the Father, seated with the court of heaven, will watch as they resist Him in futility.

> He who sits in the heavens shall laugh; the LORD shall hold them in derision. Then He shall speak to them in His wrath, and distress them in His deep displeasure.
>
> —PSALM 2:4–5

He will hand the kingdoms of the earth fully over to Jesus, the Son of Man.

> Yet I have set My King on My holy hill of Zion. I will declare the decree: The LORD has said to Me, "You are My Son, today I have begotten You. Ask of Me, and I will give You the nations for Your inheritance, and the ends of the earth for Your possession."
>
> —PSALM 2:6–8

Jesus will then return in the brightness of His glory and "shall break them with a rod of iron" (Ps. 2:9).

Just when the Antichrist thinks he has won, everything will

change: "I saw heaven opened, and behold, a white horse. And He who sat on him was called Faithful and True, and in righteousness He judges and makes war" (Rev. 19:11). "Then the heavens receded like a scroll when it is rolled up, and every mountain and island was moved from its place. Then the kings of the earth and the great men and the rich men and the commanding officers and the strong and everyone, slave and free, hid themselves in the caves and in the rocks of the mountains. They said to the mountains and rocks, 'Fall on us, and hide us from the face of Him who sits on the throne, and from the wrath of the Lamb, for the great day of His wrath has come. Who is able to withstand it?'" (Rev. 6:14–17, MEV).

> His eyes were like a flame of fire, and on His head were many crowns. He had a name written that no one knew except Himself. He was clothed with a robe dipped in blood, and His name is called The Word of God. And the armies in heaven, clothed in fine linen, white and clean, followed Him on white horses. Now out of His mouth goes a sharp sword, that with it He should strike the nations. And He Himself will rule them with a rod of iron. He Himself treads the winepress of the fierceness and wrath of Almighty God. And He has on His robe and on His thigh a name written: KING OF KINGS AND LORD OF LORDS.
>
> —REVELATION 19:12–16

Jesus as the Son of Man will lead the armies of heaven to destroy the Antichrist and his kingdom. We will rule and reign together with Him on this earth a thousand years. After the thousand years, there will be another season in which Satan will be released onto the earth, and then the lake of fire, the final judgment.

Jesus, being fully God and fully man, will be given an everlasting kingdom. We do not yet completely understand what this will look like, but we have the hope that the Son of Man is coming again. John encourages us about this in his first epistle.

Beloved, now we are children of God; and it has not yet been revealed what we shall be, but we know that when He is revealed, we shall be like Him, for we shall see Him as He is. And everyone who has this hope in Him purifies himself, just as He is pure.

—1 John 3:2–3

Prayer

Father, my hope and expectation is the soon return of Jesus as the Son of Man. Fill me with the strong confidence in this life that the absolute rulership of Your kingdom is coming again. Keep me from all deception of the enemy and fill my heart with the love of the truth. I declare, "Your kingdom come and Your will be done, on earth as it is in heaven." In Jesus' holy name, amen.

Day 19
THE ROBE OF A
HIGH PRIEST

And in the midst of the seven lampstands One like the
Son of Man, clothed with a garment down to the feet
and girded about the chest with a golden band.
—REVELATION 1:13

T HE GARMENT JOHN saw on Jesus had a golden band and was
the garment of a high priest. We have studied the need for the
shed blood of Jesus to fully redeem man, and now we see Jesus as
the eternal High Priest who offered His own blood for our sins,
not the blood of an animal.

> But Christ came as High Priest of the good things to
> come, with the greater and more perfect tabernacle not
> made with hands, that is, not of this creation. Not with
> the blood of goats and calves, but with His own blood He
> entered the Most Holy Place once for all, having obtained
> eternal redemption.
>
> —HEBREWS 9:11–12

To enter the tabernacle, the priest had to wear special holy garments. Then the high priest went into the place where God's glory
was manifest in the cloud.

> So you shall speak to all who are gifted artisans…that
> they may make Aaron's garments, to consecrate him, that
> he may minister to Me as priest. And these are the gar-
> ments which they shall make: a breastplate, an ephod, a
> robe, a skillfully woven tunic, a turban, and a sash. So
> they shall make holy garments for Aaron your brother
> and his sons, that he may minister to Me as priest.
>
> —EXODUS 28:3–4

The priestly garments were designed to be holy garments that would consecrate the priests so they could minister to God. The word *consecrate* is of specific importance that goes directly to the revelation we receive about seeing Jesus in this garment.

Consecrate means "to be sacred, consecrated, i.e., dedicate to service and loyalty to God, and so involving proper conduct (as prescribed) of any person or object so dedicated...set apart...be holy, i.e., be in a state of having superior moral qualities, with behavior which is positively unique and pure, in contrast to other corrupt standards."[1]

When we see Jesus as He is, we also see ourselves, as He is making us in His image. There are entire scholarly works about the priestly garments, but I want to focus on one main prophetic insight. Remember, the purpose of this revelation of Jesus was to prepare a people of the future for the most intense season the world would ever face. Each revelation of Jesus was given to empower us, strengthen us, and call us up to a higher spiritual experience of living like Jesus in His strength, His victory, His righteousness, and His calling. (See Ephesians 1:18.)

The aspect of the garment I want to focus on is the purity and consecration of those who minister continually before the throne of God. Those who came close to God had to be consecrated. They had to be set apart from the rest of the people. They had to be purified. Only the holy could come before God's presence.

There are many erroneous teachings today that pervert the truth of Jesus as the High Priest who presented His blood on the altar of God so that we could be deemed not guilty for our sins. They conclude that since Jesus went to heaven "by His own blood" and "entered the Most Holy Place once for all, having obtained eternal redemption" (Heb. 9:12, MEV), then that must be all that He will do. They basically teach that since all our sins are paid for, we don't ever have to worry about sin. We are free from having to live a holy life. We couldn't do it, so Jesus did it. That settles it, and now I can live my life as I see fit.

Jesus did present His blood *once* for all, but He also remains "a priest forever, in the order of Melchizedek" (Heb. 7:21, MEV). Just as the job of the high priest was not only to present the blood of the sacrificial lamb for the atonement of sins but also to minister continually to and before the Father, so too does Jesus, our eternal High Priest.

We are called as a kingdom of priests, and we are partners with Jesus in this eternal calling. The robe speaks of the purity that is required to stand in the holy of holies before the glory of God. This perfection, purity, and holiness is only available to us and imputed to us by the blood of Jesus. The priestly robe that John saw at Jesus' feet in Revelation 1:13 also speaks of consecration and separation.

The consecration involves actions that flow from this holiness produced by the blood of Jesus. Consecration means to be in a state of having superior moral qualities, with behavior that is positively unique and pure, in contrast to other corrupt standards. There was a requirement for those who came before God as priests to have a different attitude and lifestyle set apart and unique.

When the sons of Aaron came before the presence of God with strange fire, they were judged. Why? God's response to Aaron revealed a deep truth that endures today.

> By those who come near Me I must be regarded as holy;
> and before all the people I must be glorified.
> —LEVITICUS 10:3

When God spoke these words, He declared an eternal truth. Those who come near to Him must not treat Him as common. They must regard Him as sacred, holy, and worthy of special treatment; removed from common use; subject to special treatment.[2]

We live in a day when we have removed much of the sacred from our worship and ministry before God. In our desire to experience the amazing truths of Hebrews 4:16—"Let us therefore come boldly to the throne of grace"—we have forgotten that "since we are receiving a kingdom which cannot be shaken, let us have grace, by which we may serve God acceptably with reverence and godly fear. For our God is a consuming fire" (Heb. 12:28–29).

The early church had the balance of the boldness to come before God with open arms and to do it with the fear of the Lord.

> Then the churches throughout all Judea, Galilee, and Samaria had peace and were edified. And walking in the fear of the Lord and in the comfort of the Holy Spirit, they were multiplied.
>
> —Acts 9:31

The priestly robe of Jesus reminds us not only that He cleansed us of our sins but also that He called us to live a set-apart life distinctly different from the standards of the world so that we can minister to the Father.

The blood of Jesus has cleansed us but also continues to cleanse us. The blood gives us access to serve God with fear, reverence, awe, and a recognition that He is worthy of our wholeheartedness. We are forgiven and washed, but we are also required to continue in the light of the knowledge of the glory of God as revealed in the face of Jesus.

> But if we walk in the light as He is in the light, we have fellowship with one another, and the blood of Jesus Christ His Son cleanses us from all sin.
>
> —1 John 1:7

The verb translated "cleanses" (καθαρίζει) means not only to forgive but also to remove. The cleansing is present and continuous.[3] I see it as an eternal flow of the blood of Christ continually washing me as I remain in Him. The unique part about this verse is that the continual cleansing is directly connected to our continuing to "walk in the light as He is in the light" (1 John 1:7, MEV).

Several analogies in the New Testament describe this need for continual connection to remain in the life flow given by the blood of Jesus.

> I am the vine, you are the branches. He who abides in Me, and I in him, bears much fruit; for without Me you

can do nothing. If anyone does not abide in Me, he is cast out as a branch and is withered; and they gather them and throw them into the fire, and they are burned. If you abide in Me, and My words abide in you, you will ask what you desire, and it shall be done for you....As the Father loved Me, I also have loved you; abide in My love.

—JOHN 15:5–7, 9

For it is impossible for those who were once enlightened, and have tasted the heavenly gift, and have become partakers of the Holy Spirit, and have tasted the good word of God and the powers of the age to come, if they fall away, to renew them again to repentance, since they crucify again for themselves the Son of God, and put Him to an open shame.

—HEBREWS 6:4–6

Of how much worse punishment, do you suppose, will he be thought worthy who has trampled the Son of God underfoot, counted the blood of the covenant by which he was sanctified a common thing, and insulted the Spirit of grace?

—HEBREWS 10:29

Specifically note the words "counted the blood of the covenant...a common thing." This is where we find the problem and what this aspect of the robe speaks to us today. The robe was to separate, consecrate, and set the priest apart for sacred worship and ministry unto God.

In Ezekiel 44, a great sin occurred during the Babylonian captivity. God told the prophet to speak to the priests "because they ministered to them before their idols and caused the house of Israel to fall into iniquity, therefore I have lifted up My hand against them, says the Lord GOD, that they shall bear the punishment of their iniquity" (Ezek. 44:12, MEV).

These priests had compromised with the spirit of the day. They had in essence embraced the heathen culture of Babylon and mixed it with the worship of God, thus causing the children of Israel to fall into sin. The priests' failure to keep the worship of God pure brought a great judgment. I think this judgment is one of the most devastating punishments that any of us, as a kingdom of priests, could bear. God said, "They shall not come near to Me to do the office of a priest to Me, nor to come near to any of My holy things in the Most Holy Place. But they shall bear their shame and their abominations which they have committed" (Ezek. 44:13, MEV).

When we take for granted the shed blood of Jesus and walk in man's ways and not God's ways, we are in danger of being separated from the greatest ministry of all: being a kingdom of priests who have the honor and privilege to minister before the glory of God.

There are those who claim that since Jesus came, we all have unlimited access to the holy of holies no matter how we live. This is a grave error and has led to much loss in the body of Christ.

Idolatry is the worship of an image of God that is not God. It might be a carved image, but it can also be a false concept of God. Idolatry worships an *image* created by man. The guilty priests were no longer allowed to come into the tabernacle to minister before God's manifested presence because they (the priests) had also ministered to the people "before their idols." Thus, they worshipped and presented a false image of God. They polluted the worship of God with the culture of the day.

The sons of the priest Zadok were different. They kept the worship and ministry of God sacred. Look at what God says about them.

> "But the priests, the Levites, the sons of Zadok, who kept charge of My sanctuary when the children of Israel went astray from Me, they shall come near Me to minister to Me; and they shall stand before Me to offer to Me the fat and the blood," says the Lord GOD. "They shall enter My sanctuary, and they shall come near My table to minister to Me, and they shall keep My charge."
>
> —EZEKIEL 44:15–16

They were given specific instructions on how they were to come before God: "...when they enter at the gates of the inner court, they shall be clothed with linen garments" (Ezek. 44:17, MEV).

This is the foundational piece of the garment that John saw Jesus wearing: the white linen priestly robe. The priests were required to wear this robe of consecration and separation to come before God to minister to Him. Only the priests were allowed to wear this garment, and only when they ministered before God, not when they ministered to the people.

> When they go out to the outer court, to the outer court to the people, they shall take off their garments in which they have ministered, leave them in the holy chambers, and put on other garments; and in their holy garments they shall not sanctify the people.
>
> —EZEKIEL 44:19

The compromising priests were never allowed to put on holy garments again and minister to God. They were only allowed to minister to the people. God said this of the compromising priests:

> "Yet they shall be ministers in My sanctuary, as gate-keepers of the house and ministers of the house; they shall slay the burnt offering and the sacrifice for the people, and they shall stand before them to minister to them. Because they ministered to them before their idols and caused the house of Israel to fall into iniquity, therefore I have raised My hand in an oath against them," says the Lord GOD, "that they shall bear their iniquity. And they shall not come near Me to minister to Me as priest, nor come near any of My holy things, nor into the Most Holy Place; but they shall bear their shame and their abominations which they have committed. Nevertheless I will make them keep charge of the temple, for all its work, and for all that has to be done in it."
>
> —EZEKIEL 44:11–14

This is one of the most devastating results of compromise that is still being played out today. God may allow a minister to flow in the gifts of the Spirit, minister to the people, and do the work of ministry, but they might have lost the deep, divine connection needed to come before the manifested presence of God to minister to Him. I have talked with many supposedly anointed ministers who are far from God. They have told me in private that they are so distant from Him that they feel dry and dead, their prayers are lifeless, and they have lost intimacy with God. This happens because we forget about the holy garments available to us by the blood of Jesus, but we also forget that ministering before God requires a separation from the world.

When we see Jesus standing as the Son of Man in the midst of the seven golden lampstands with a garment at His feet, we are to recognize our holy calling to join Jesus as priests. We are to focus on the calling to be consecrated unto God and not to mix the holy and unholy. God's instruction to the sons of Zadok, who kept the worship pure, was that "they shall teach My people the difference between the holy and profane, and cause them to discern between the unclean and the clean" (Ezek. 44:23, MEV).

God said, "I will be sanctified by those who come near Me; and before all the people I will be glorified" (Lev. 10:3, MEV). This requirement to come reverentially before God's presence is one of the most forsaken truths of modern Christianity, and I believe this has led to the weakness of much of the Christian church.

The end-time saints will regain an awe and reverence of coming before God with fear and trembling, filled with the revelation of being the bride of Christ in pursuit of the deepest intimacy with holy fear.

> The secret [of the sweet, satisfying companionship] of the Lord have they who fear (revere and worship) Him, and He will show them His covenant and reveal to them its [deep, inner] meaning.
>
> —PSALM 25:14, AMPC

David penned these amazing words while running for his life from King Saul:

> They looked to Him and were radiant, and their faces were not ashamed....The angel of the LORD encamps all around those who fear Him, and delivers them. Oh, taste and see that the LORD is good; blessed is the man who trusts in Him! Oh, fear the LORD, you His saints! There is no want to those who fear Him. The young lions lack and suffer hunger; but those who seek the LORD shall not lack any good thing. Come, you children, listen to me; I will teach you the fear of the LORD.
> —PSALM 34:5, 7–11

God reveals Himself to those who worship Him in the fear of the Lord, those who do not treat the Lord and His presence as common but instead separate themselves from the spirit of the day, put on holy garments, and come before Him in awe. These worshippers who worship in spirit and truth shall minister unto Him. They shall see His beauty and glory, and they shall be the ones who truly taste and see the Lord's goodness, which is His glory.

God promises:

> "I will dwell in them and walk among them. I will be their God, and they shall be My people." Therefore "Come out from among them and be separate, says the Lord. Do not touch what is unclean, and I will receive you."...Therefore, having these promises, beloved, let us cleanse ourselves from all filthiness of the flesh and spirit, perfecting holiness in the fear of God.
> —2 CORINTHIANS 6:16–17; 7:1

Prayer

Father, consecrate me unto Yourself. Cause me to draw near to You in holiness and godly fear. I receive from You white garments, that I may be clothed and the shame of my nakedness may not be revealed. I choose to honor and revere You in all I say and do. Separate me from the spirit of the world and purify my worship. Anoint me to behold You in Your glory. In Jesus' holy name, amen.

Day 20
JESUS' ABSOLUTE AUTHORITY, WISDOM, PURITY, AND JUDGMENT

His head and hair were white like wool, as white as snow.
—REVELATION 1:14

THIS IS WHERE the revelation of Jesus clearly identifies with God the Father. John's mind must have been filled with the images of Daniel's vision.

> I watched till thrones were put in place, and the Ancient of Days was seated; His garment was white as snow, and the hair of His head was like pure wool. His throne was a fiery flame.
>
> —DANIEL 7:9

Jesus wore the same garment—a linen robe as white as snow. The hair of His head was pure like wool. The interchangeable use of *white* and *pure* points us to this revelation.

> His head and hair were white like wool, as white as snow, and His eyes like a flame of fire.
>
> —REVELATION 1:14

This vision of Daniel is the first place where white is attributed to God. The law of first mention applies strongly here. Jesus' "head and hair were white like wool, as white as snow," the same as the Father's. This reveals four attributes of Jesus: His absolute authority, His absolute wisdom, His absolute purity, and His absolute authority as judge.

The scene is important. God comes to the court of heaven ready to oversee and judge the earth. "The court was seated, and the books were opened" (Dan. 7:10).

JESUS' ABSOLUTE AUTHORITY

Jesus, as the Son of Man and the Son of God, is one with the Father as a full member of the Trinity. The Godhead, being Three in One, is also three distinct persons. Seeing Jesus with the same description as the Father, with His head and hair being white, reveals His oneness with the Ancient of Days. Because the law of first mention applies, we ascribe to Jesus the same authority, wisdom, purity, and righteous judgment that God the Father possesses.

In Daniel's vision, Jesus as the Son of Man comes with the clouds of heaven. "He came to the Ancient of Days and was presented before Him. There was given to Him dominion, and glory, and a kingdom, that all peoples, nations, and languages should serve Him. His dominion is an everlasting dominion, which shall not pass away, and His kingdom that which shall not be destroyed" (Dan. 7:13–14, MEV).

Jesus says, "All authority has been given to Me in heaven and on earth" (Matt. 28:18, MEV). The word *authority* is from the Greek word *exousia*, which in this context generally means the right to exercise God's power; the right to judge, rule, and act with God's supernatural power.[1]

Jesus has the legal right to exercise all the power of heaven over all creation. Everything is under His domain, and He has absolute supernatural power over everything. There is no devil, no demon, no sickness, no natural event, no evil empire, and no plot of the wicked that He does not have total right to judge and exercise all the power of heaven against.

Through the cross, Jesus absolutely defeated the works of the enemy. "For this purpose the Son of God was revealed, that He might destroy the works of the devil" (1 John 3:8, MEV). I like how the Amplified Bible, Classic Edition puts it: "The reason the Son of God was made manifest (visible) was to undo (destroy, loosen, and dissolve) the works the devil [has done]."

Jesus has received all power and authority from His Father. "Therefore God highly exalted Him and gave Him the name which is above every name, that at the name of Jesus every knee should bow, of those in heaven and on earth and under the earth, and every tongue should confess that Jesus Christ is Lord, to the glory of God the Father" (Phil. 2:9–11, MEV).

Jesus' power and authority aren't just barely superior to evil. Jesus' power over all the works of the devil is so utterly superior that Psalms says, "The Lord will laugh at him, for He sees that his day is coming" (Ps. 37:13, MEV).

> Yours, O LORD, is the greatness, the power and the glory, the victory and the majesty; for all that is in heaven and in earth is Yours; Yours is the kingdom, O LORD, and You are exalted as head over all. Both riches and honor come from You, and You reign over all. In Your hand is power and might; in Your hand it is to make great and to give strength to all.
>
> —1 CHRONICLES 29:11–12

JESUS' ABSOLUTE WISDOM

> He counts the number of the stars; He calls them all by name. Great is our Lord, and mighty in power; His understanding is infinite. The LORD lifts up the humble; He casts the wicked down to the ground.
>
> —PSALM 147:4–6

> Oh, the depth of the riches both of the wisdom and knowledge of God! How unsearchable are His judgments and His ways past finding out! *"For who has known the mind of the Lord? Or who has become His counselor?"*
>
> —ROMANS 11:33–34, EMPHASIS ADDED

"Christ the power of God and the wisdom of God" (1 Cor. 1:24) "in whom are hidden all the treasures of wisdom and knowledge" (Col. 2:3, MEV).

The word *wisdom* means "the capacity to understand, and hence act wisely."[2] Jesus has the absolute capacity to understand; therefore, He acts in the wisest way possible. The white head speaks of wisdom that comes from age and experience. God is called the Ancient of Days in this first description of God as having white hair. When we see Jesus given the same description, it tells us that Jesus has the same eternal wisdom that comes from the fact that He always existed.

Jesus' wisdom is so far beyond that of any human that Paul says, "The foolishness of God is wiser than men, and the weakness of God is stronger than men" (1 Cor. 1:25, MEV). We can put our total trust in Jesus and in the plan that He is working out in our lives. Even though it may seem like everything is collapsing around us, we can trust and rest in His wisdom. He knows exactly what He is doing and exactly how to execute His plan.

> "For My thoughts are not your thoughts, nor are your ways My ways," says the LORD. "For as the heavens are higher than the earth, so are My ways higher than your ways, and My thoughts than your thoughts."
>
> —ISAIAH 55:8–9

Focusing on Jesus' absolute wisdom brings us peace. "You will guard him and keep him in perfect and constant peace whose mind [both its inclination and its character] is stayed on You, because he commits himself to You, leans on You, and hopes confidently in You. So trust in the Lord (commit yourself to Him, lean on Him, hope confidently in Him) forever; for the Lord God is an everlasting Rock [the Rock of Ages] (Isa. 26:3–4, AMPC).

Jesus is wisdom. Look at the promises and workings of wisdom from Proverbs 8.

> I, wisdom, dwell with prudence, and find out knowledge and discretion. The fear of the LORD is to hate evil; pride and arrogance and the evil way....Counsel is mine, and sound wisdom; I am understanding, I have strength. By me kings reign, and rulers decree justice. By me princes

rule, and nobles, all the judges of the earth. I love those who love me, and those who seek me diligently will find me. Riches and honor are with me, enduring riches and righteousness. My fruit is better than gold, yes, than fine gold, and my revenue than choice silver.

I traverse the way of righteousness, in the midst of the paths of justice, that I may cause those who love me to inherit wealth, that I may fill their treasuries....I have been established from everlasting, from the beginning, before there was ever an earth....When He prepared the heavens, I was there, when He drew a circle on the face of the deep, when He established the clouds above, when He strengthened the fountains of the deep, when He assigned to the sea its limit, so that the waters would not transgress His command, when He marked out the foundations of the earth, then I was beside Him as a master craftsman; and I was daily His delight, rejoicing always before Him, rejoicing in His inhabited world, and my delight was with the sons of men.

Now therefore, listen to me, my children, for blessed are those who keep my ways. Hear instruction and be wise, and do not disdain it. Blessed is the man who listens to me, watching daily at my gates, waiting at the posts of my doors. For whoever finds me finds life, and obtains favor from the LORD.

—PROVERBS 8:12–21, 23, 27–35

JESUS' ABSOLUTE PURITY

But with the precious blood of Christ, as of a lamb without blemish and without spot.

—1 PETER 1:19

For we do not have a High Priest who cannot sympathize with our weaknesses, but was in all points tempted as we are, yet without sin.

—HEBREWS 4:15

Jesus lived a sinless life here on the earth by the same Holy Spirit that He gave to us. His purity extended to us through the Holy Spirit. He did not just forgive us. He made it possible for us to access all the power needed to live a godly life. "Grace and peace be multiplied to you in the knowledge of God and of Jesus our Lord, as His divine power has given to us all things that pertain to life and godliness, through the knowledge of Him who called us by glory and virtue" (2 Pet. 1:2–3).

Peter says that all things we need for godliness have been given to us through the knowledge of Jesus. As we affix our attention on Him and see Him as perfectly pure, we too can live in His purity. The promise of the power to overcome sin and be pure is found throughout the New Testament, but it requires us to behold Him. We are transformed into His purity of thought and action because our minds and spirits are continually filled with the revelation knowledge of who He is and what He is focused on.

> And all of us, as with unveiled face, [because we] continued to behold [in the Word of God] as in a mirror the glory of the Lord, are constantly being transfigured into His very own image in ever increasing splendor and from one degree of glory to another; [for this comes] from the Lord [Who is] the Spirit.
>
> —2 Corinthians 3:18, ampc

As our minds are stayed on Him, we are renewed into His image; therefore, "do not be conformed to this world, but be transformed by the renewing of your mind" (Rom. 12:2, mev). The promise of the Holy Spirit, whose job is to reveal Jesus, is to empower you to "walk in the Spirit, and you shall not fulfill the lust of the flesh" (Gal. 5:16, mev).

Jesus' Absolute Authority to Judge

> I was watching in the night visions, and behold, One like the Son of Man, coming with the clouds of heaven! He came to the Ancient of Days, and they brought Him

near before Him. Then to Him was given dominion and glory and a kingdom, that all peoples, nations, and languages should serve Him. His dominion is an everlasting dominion....

I was watching; and the same horn was making war against the saints, and prevailing against them, until the Ancient of Days came, and a judgment was made in favor of the saints of the Most High, and the time came for the saints to possess the kingdom.

—DANIEL 7:13–14, 21–22

This description of Jesus with His head and hair white like wool and white as snow, referring to His exact likeness of the Father, is first seen in Daniel 7 when the power of the Antichrist is utterly destroyed. The court is seated, and final judgment is made. Even though there will be a short time when it will seem like the devil is winning, the final judgments have already been written.

Then the saints shall be given into his hand for a time and times and half a time. But the court shall be seated, and they shall take away his dominion, to consume and destroy it forever. Then the kingdom and dominion, and the greatness of the kingdoms under the whole heaven, shall be given to the people, the saints of the Most High. His kingdom is an everlasting kingdom, and all dominions shall serve and obey Him.

—DANIEL 7:25–27

When we see Jesus with absolute authority, wisdom, purity, and judgment, we can have unshakable confidence through any and all circumstances. The victory is guaranteed. Wickedness will eventually be utterly defeated, and all the kingdoms will be delivered to Him and to the saints. Yes, all the kingdoms under heaven are being given to us through Jesus.

We are to see Jesus as one with the Ancient of Days. He is the righteous judge filled with eternal wisdom. His judgments are pure, true, and altogether righteous.

Jesus reveals to John that even though this horrible evil is coming, Jesus will judge in favor of the saints as the King and righteous judge.

> I was watching; and the same horn [Antichrist] was making war against the saints, and prevailing against them, until the Ancient of Days came, and a judgment was made in favor of the saints of the Most High, and the time came for the saints to possess the kingdom.
>
> —DANIEL 7:21–22

Prayer

Father, in Jesus the Son of Man is all authority, wisdom, purity, and righteous judgments. As I am united in Christ, cause the fullness of Jesus to be manifest in and through my life. Exercise Your authority, flood me with Your wisdom, purify me as refined gold, and teach me to walk in Your righteous judgments. In Jesus' holy name, amen.

Day 21
EYES LIKE FIRE, PART 1

His head and hair were white like wool, as white
as snow, and His eyes like a flame of fire.
—REVELATION 1:14

O F ALL THE descriptions of Jesus, this is by far my favorite.
It is hard to establish any one description over another, as
they are all equally and fully balanced, but each person will find
some that speak to him or her more than others. I believe this
description will become much more strongly emphasized in the
last days. Therefore, I am going to spend the greatest number of
days on Jesus' eyes of fire.

The eyes of God see everything. "And not a creature exists that
is concealed from His sight, but all things are open and exposed,
naked and defenseless to the eyes of Him with Whom we have to
do" (Heb. 4:13, AMPC).

Nothing is hidden from God's sight. He sees all and is completely aware of everything. There isn't a single moment of your
life, your thoughts, your sufferings, or your responses to God in
righteousness that He doesn't see. Psalm 139 is an incredible over-
view of the effects of God's eyes that see everything.

> O LORD, You have searched me and known me. You know
> my sitting down and my rising up; You understand my
> thought afar off. You comprehend my path and my lying
> down, and are acquainted with all my ways. For there is
> not a word on my tongue, but behold, O LORD, You know
> it altogether....Where can I go from Your Spirit? Or where
> can I flee from Your presence? If I ascend into heaven, You
> are there; if I make my bed in hell, behold, You are there....
>
> For You formed my inward parts; You covered me in
> my mother's womb. I will praise You, for I am fearfully
> and wonderfully made; marvelous are Your works, and

that my soul knows very well. My frame was not hidden
from You, when I was made in secret, and skillfully
wrought in the lowest parts of the earth.

—Psalm 139:1–4, 7–8, 13–15

God's eyes were focused on you even while He was forming
you in your mother's womb. He was skillfully and wonderfully
forming you in intricate beauty.

In 2019 I entered Yosemite Valley on a beautiful spring
morning. I was awed by the beauty of the towering granite cliffs,
the majestic waterfalls, the lush valley floor, and the sounds of
the morning birds singing a hallelujah chorus. It was one of those
scenes that seem to freeze time. As I looked upon such incredible
beauty, I said to the Lord, "How much joy it must have brought
You to create the individual beauty of each of these."

The Lord then spoke to me and said, "It is nothing in compar-
ison to the joy I experienced when I created the unique beauty of
every single human being." I was struck to my heart with these
piercing words. I immediately felt the incredible love of God for
every human and my complete lack of properly seeing people as
God sees them. I cried out, "God, help me see the beauty of each
and every person the way You see them."

David continues with this revelation of the eyes of God.

Your eyes saw my substance, being yet unformed. And in
Your book they all were written, the days fashioned for
me, when as yet there were none of them.

—Psalm 139:16

David reveals that every day of our lives has already been seen
by God. This great mystery of God has baffled scholars throughout
the centuries. How can we have a free will if God already wrote
in a book all the days that were fashioned for us? Some take a
very Calvinistic approach and say God sovereignly controls all the
actions of every person. Others say it is simply because God lives
outside of time and therefore sees the end from the beginning.

Without getting stuck in a theological debate, I want to focus on a particular truth: that God is so intimately involved in our everyday lives that He knows each day before it happens.

This great truth gives us amazing comfort because it reassures us that God has never left us or forsaken us. He is involved in our every decision and action. His eyes are focused on us day and night.

> How precious also are Your thoughts to me, O God! How great is the sum of them! If I should count them, they would be more in number than the sand; when I awake, I am still with You.
>
> —PSALM 139:17–18

You and I are not afterthoughts to God. We consume His mind and heart; we are ever before Him.

> Many, O LORD my God, are Your wonderful works which You have done; and Your thoughts toward us cannot be recounted to You in order; if I would declare and speak of them, they are more than can be numbered.
>
> —PSALM 40:5

His thoughts toward us are driven by His love. He desires the best for all of us and is actively working those ends as we yield to Him.

> For I know the thoughts that I think toward you, says the LORD, thoughts of peace and not of evil, to give you a future and a hope.
>
> —JEREMIAH 29:11

His eyes do not only look upon us with the hope to bless us. God also sees the wickedness done to us. He is not blind to the evil that men do.

> The eyes of the LORD are in every place, keeping watch on the evil and the good.
>
> —PROVERBS 15:3

> For the eyes of the LORD are on the righteous, and His
> ears are open to their prayers; but the face of the LORD is
> against those who do evil.
>
> —1 PETER 3:12

One of the great strategies of the enemy is to get us to feel alone. Depression, discouragement, loneliness, shame, and many self-destructive behaviors flow from feelings of isolation. When we fail to keep our eyes on His eyes, we lose sight of heaven's reality. Man's reality and heaven's reality are often far apart. Man's reality is based on temporary circumstances, but heaven's reality is based on the truth that God is working a master plan.

> "For My thoughts are not your thoughts, nor are your
> ways My ways," says the LORD. "For as the heavens are
> higher than the earth, so are My ways higher than your
> ways, and My thoughts than your thoughts."
>
> —ISAIAH 55:8–9

God's workings are often strange to us, and many of them do not make sense to the human mind. We can trust in and rely on the truth that God sees everything. Nothing has happened that has missed His attention. With Jesus' having this ultimate vision and being the One filled with eternal wisdom, "we know that all things work together for good to those who love God, to those who are called according to His purpose" (Rom. 8:28, MEV).

This description of Jesus is not merely about His all-seeing eyes; rather, His eyes as described in Revelation were like flames of fire. This brings a whole new level of understanding that the Father wanted Jesus to reveal to us about Himself.

We will focus on three areas of Jesus' eyes of fire in the coming days:

1. Jesus' fiery, passionate desire

2. The purifying fire of Jesus' holiness

3. The fire of God's judgment

Fire is an important description of God that reveals to us His nature. If we fail to see God as a God of fire, we will fail to understand much of what He does in our lives and in the events of the world. God is surrounded by fire.

> And the Angel of the LORD appeared to him *in a flame of fire* from the midst of a bush. So he looked, and behold, the bush was burning with fire, but the bush was not consumed.
> —EXODUS 3:2, EMPHASIS ADDED

God spoke to Moses out of the fire and connected the manifestation of the fire with His holiness. As Moses drew near to the burning bush, God spoke: "Do not draw near this place. Take your sandals off your feet, for the place where you stand is holy ground" (Exod. 3:5).

> When the sun had gone down and a [thick] darkness had come on, behold, *a smoking oven and a flaming torch passed between those pieces.*
> —GENESIS 15:17, AMPC, EMPHASIS ADDED

> Now Mount Sinai was completely in smoke, because *the LORD descended upon it in fire.*
> —EXODUS 19:18, EMPHASIS ADDED

> Now the glory of the LORD rested on Mount Sinai, and the cloud covered it six days. And on the seventh day He called to Moses out of the midst of the cloud. *The sight of the glory of the LORD was like a consuming fire on the top of the mountain in the eyes of the children of Israel.* So Moses went into the midst of the cloud and went up into the mountain. And Moses was on the mountain forty days and forty nights.
> —EXODUS 24:16–18, EMPHASIS ADDED

God appeared to Abram as fire, He appeared to Moses as fire, and He appeared to the children of Israel as fire. Fire also played a huge part in the tabernacle. The offerings were consumed by fire.

The oil was burned in the candlestick by fire. Fire was added to the incense that produced the cloud that God's glory filled.

> The LORD reigns; let the earth rejoice; let the multitude of isles be glad! Clouds and darkness surround Him; righteousness and justice are the foundation of His throne. *A fire goes before Him, and burns up His enemies round about.*
> —PSALM 97:1–3, EMPHASIS ADDED

> "Is not *My word like a fire?*" says the LORD, "And like a hammer that breaks the rock in pieces?"
> —JEREMIAH 23:29, EMPHASIS ADDED

GOD'S THRONE IS A FIERY FLAME

> I watched till thrones were put in place, and the Ancient of Days was seated; His garment was white as snow, and the hair of His head was like pure wool. *His throne was a fiery flame,* its wheels a burning fire; *a fiery stream issued and came forth from before Him.* A thousand thousands ministered to Him; ten thousand times ten thousand stood before Him. The court was seated, and the books were opened.
> —DANIEL 7:9–10, EMPHASIS ADDED

> John answered, saying to all, "I indeed baptize you with water; but One mightier than I is coming, whose sandal strap I am not worthy to loose. *He will baptize you with the Holy Spirit and fire.* His winnowing fan is in His hand, and He will thoroughly clean out His threshing floor, and gather the wheat into His barn; but the chaff He will burn with *unquenchable fire.*"
> —LUKE 3:16–17, EMPHASIS ADDED

When we think of Jesus' eyes of fire today, let us meditate on the truth that God sees everything. His eyes of fire are focused on every detail of our lives. His eyes of fire reveal His holiness, His glory, and the intensity of His passion for us. No matter how evil these days become, there is nothing out of His sight and nothing that His eyes of fire do not see.

Remember, "the eyes of the LORD are on the righteous, and His ears are open to their cry. The face of the LORD is against the ones doing evil, to cut off the memory of them from the earth. The righteous cry out, and the LORD hears, and delivers them out of all their troubles" (Ps. 34:15–17, MEV).

Prayer

Father, You are a consuming fire. Jesus, Your eyes of fire see everything. You know me altogether. Not a thought or action of mine escapes Your gaze. Your love is so complete toward me that it is as a fire. Consume me in Your love and burn out of me everything that stands between or hinders our love relationship. In Jesus' holy name, amen.

Day 22
EYES LIKE FIRE, PART 2

His eyes were like a flame of fire, and on
His head were many crowns.

—REVELATION 19:12

THE GREATEST REVELATION of all that will keep us in these troubling days is the revelation of Jesus' eyes of fiery, passionate desire for us. It is hard for many of us to see God with deep, passionate emotions. We tend to think of emotions as mainly a human experience, especially passionate emotions, but we are emotional because God is emotional.

Man was created unique above all other creations. We were specifically created to interact with God in the deepest and most intimate way. We were specifically designed by God to be the bride of Christ, a bride who could fully engage, participate, and interact with her Bridegroom, Jesus.

God placed within us the capacity to interact with Him spiritually, emotionally, and physically. "Then God said, 'Let us make man in our image, after our likeness'" (Gen. 1:26, MEV). All the other created beings God made according to their own kind. "So God made the beasts of the earth according to their kind, and the livestock according to their kind, and everything that creeps on the earth according to its kind. And God saw that it was good" (Gen. 1:25, MEV). Ten times in Genesis 1 God said He created the grasses, birds, herbs, cattle, beasts, and all animals according to their own kind, but He created man after His own likeness.

David represented this uniqueness when he said, "What is man that You are mindful of him, and the son of man that You attend to him? For You have made him a little lower than the angels, and crowned him with glory and honor. You have given him dominion over the works of Your hands; You have put all things under his feet" (Ps. 8:4–6, MEV).

The Father's unique purpose for creating man to be the bride of Christ and to share with us all that He is and all that He has for all eternity is pivotal for us to understand and to grasp why Jesus has such passionate, fiery desire for us.

The first place in the Bible where God is described as fire (and not just seen in fire) is Deuteronomy 4:24: "For the LORD your God is a consuming fire, a jealous God."

The description of God being a consuming fire is directly connected to the intensity of the emotion described as "jealous."

The word *jealous* means "fiercely protective and unaccepting of disloyalty."[1] In the Book of Exodus, God describes Himself as jealous. This description gives us greater insight into the nature of godly jealousy.

> But you shall destroy their altars, break their sacred pillars, and cut down their wooden images (for you shall worship no other god, for the LORD, whose name is Jealous, is a jealous God), lest you make a covenant with the inhabitants of the land, and they play the harlot with their gods and make sacrifice to their gods, and one of them invites you and you eat of his sacrifice, and you take of his daughters for your sons, and his daughters play the harlot with their gods and make your sons play the harlot with their gods.
> —EXODUS 34:13–16

Note the marriage covenant talk here. God is saying, "I am so in love with you, and I am jealous for your complete affection and attention. Do not 'play the harlot' with others. I want all of your love. Because I so deeply desire you, I want you to completely desire Me. My love and desire for you is so complete that it is as a consuming fire."

God's fiery, loving desire for us is so consuming that it motivates Him to eradicate everything in our lives that stands in the way of us experiencing the fullness of this love. He wants to remove every sin, every distraction, and every other lover from our hearts so we can fully and completely love Him as He loves us.

Jesus' love for us is powerfully and prophetically revealed in the Song of Solomon. Although this is probably a real story described by Solomon, it is included in Scripture because it is a prophetic image of Christ's love and relationship with His bride. All Scripture reveals Jesus. Jesus is in every part of the Bible. The Song of Solomon reveals the depth and intensity of His love for us. We are His beloved.

There is such beauty in Song of Solomon chapter 4, where Jesus expresses His love for His bride. The Shulamite woman was from a farming region, so Jesus used agricultural language, and the beloved was from the temple, so He also used temple language. Look at a few verses through the lens of Jesus describing us.

> You are beautiful, my darling, beautiful beyond words. Your eyes are like doves behind your veil. Your hair falls in waves, like a flock of goats winding down the slopes of Gilead. Your teeth are as white as sheep, recently shorn and freshly washed. Your smile is flawless, each tooth matched with its twin. Your lips are like scarlet ribbon; your mouth is inviting. Your cheeks are like rosy pomegranates behind your veil. Your neck is as beautiful as the tower of David, jeweled with the shields of a thousand heroes. Your breasts are like two fawns, twin fawns of a gazelle grazing among the lilies. Before the dawn breezes blow and the night shadows flee, I will hurry to the mountain of myrrh and to the hill of frankincense. You are altogether beautiful, my darling, beautiful in every way.
>
> —SONG OF SOLOMON 4:1–7, NLT

These descriptions are full of adoration and attraction. He uses images of the beauty of nature because the Shulamite woman would understand them. He says that she is "beautiful beyond words." His attraction to her consumes His emotions.

Jesus describes what He is willing to do for her. In verse 6, He describes Calvary. The mountain of myrrh speaks of where He would be buried, and the hill of frankincense is Calvary. The Fausset and Brown commentary says, "Historically, *the hill of frankincense* is Calvary, where, 'through the eternal Spirit, He offered Himself;' the mountain of myrrh is His embalmment (Jn 19:39) till the resurrection 'daybreak.'"[2]

We are getting a glimpse of the depth of Jesus' love, the love that drove Him to go to the cross to redeem us from the land of danger. He then calls His bride to leave Lebanon, a land known for danger, and come to Him.

> Come with me from Lebanon, my bride, come with me from Lebanon. Come down from Mount Amana, from the peaks of Senir and Hermon, where the lions have their dens and leopards live among the hills.
> —SONG OF SOLOMON 4:8, NLT

He invites her twice: "Come with me from Lebanon." Jesus is calling us to come to Him where He is. He is calling us to separate ourselves, even from our family, friends, and familiar surroundings, to fully embrace Him as our spouse.

Look how these verses in Song of Solomon parallel Luke chapter 9:

> Jesus warned his disciples not to tell anyone who he was. "The Son of Man must suffer many terrible things," he said. "He will be rejected by the elders, the leading priests, and the teachers of religious law. He will be killed, but on the third day he will be raised from the dead." Then he said to the crowd, "If any of you wants to be my follower, you must give up your own way, take up your cross daily, and follow me. If you try to hang on to your life, you will lose it. But if you give up your life for my sake, you will save it."
> —LUKE 9:21–24, NLT

Jesus describes His death, burial, and resurrection, then calls His disciples to forsake everything to follow (come to) Him.

When you read Luke, think about the passionate way in which Jesus describes you in Song of Solomon: "You are beautiful, my darling, beautiful beyond words." This is Jesus talking about you and me.

Then Jesus blows my mind with what He says in Song of Solomon 4:9. This is one of my favorite passages in the whole of Scripture.

> You have ravished my heart, my sister, my spouse; you have ravished my heart with one look of your eyes, with one link of your necklace.
>
> —Song of Solomon 4:9

Jesus did not say that you ravished His heart when you lived in total obedience and perfect unity. He said, "You have ravished my heart with one look of your eyes." When I stop for just one moment and look toward Him, it ravishes His heart. When I acknowledge Him and look with affection toward Him, it ravishes His heart. Even in my weaknesses, even in my flawed love, when I look unto Him and direct my heart toward Him, Jesus says it ravishes His heart.

Through my study of the complex word *ravished* in the Hebrew, I have developed my own definition: to overwhelm with emotion; to enrapture; to give great delight to, captivate, fascinate; to overwhelm with emotions of delight because of one who is unusually attractive to God.

Through the Song of Solomon, Jesus says that with one look you captivate Him, and He is overwhelmed with emotions of delight. In other words, you ignite His eyes of fiery desire for you. Your pursuit of wholeheartedness, not when you reach the point of maturity, is what ravishes His heart.

We are desirable to Jesus even in our weaknesses. When we respond to Him and focus our attention on Him, He finds us unusually attractive. Declare that out loud to Jesus right now. "Jesus, You find me unusually attractive." It might seem weird at first, but keep doing it until it sinks deep into your spirit. When you look toward Him, see those eyes of fiery, loving desire looking at you, calling you to come to Him where He is.

> I am my beloved's, and his desire is toward me.
>
> —Song of Solomon 7:10

What an amazing statement! Jesus desires me. In His final prayer to the Father, Jesus said, "Father, I desire that they also whom You gave Me may be with Me where I am" (John 17:24). Jesus' desire for us will flood our hearts and minds so that we no longer look for the approval and acceptance of others. When we are rooted in His love and desire for us, we are delivered from the need of getting those things from people. Without this revelation we are vulnerable.

If we are not rooted in Jesus' desire for us and His enjoyment of us, we will seek approval and acceptance in all other places. As a result, we will endure so much traffic, noise, and competition in our relationship with God because we will be jockeying for position and seeking for approval outside of Him.

The revelation of God's eyes of fiery, passionate desire for us is probably the most powerful force to keep us drawing close to Him in a world that rejects everything that is holy and true. Our need for acceptance and approval from others—because we have not seen Jesus' eyes of fiery desire for us—gives the enemy inroads to derail us from the lifelong path we are on as Christians.

But when we keep our eyes on our Lord's eyes of fiery desire for us, we have the strength to overcome the rejection, heartache, suffering, and evils of this world. When we delight ourselves in Him because He delights in us, we overcome the enemy, because God's love never fails.

Prayer

Father, help me to experience the intensity of Jesus' fiery, passionate desire for me. Overflow me with the revelation of the depth of Your love and how beautiful I am to You. Deliver me from the opinions of men and fill my mind with Your passionate thoughts about me. Ignite in me the same passion for Jesus that He has for me. In Jesus' holy name, amen.

Day 23
EYES LIKE A FLAME AND FEET OF BRASS

His feet were like fine brass, as if refined in a furnace.
—REVELATION 1:15

A s WE SEE Jesus with His eyes of flaming, passionate, fiery desire, we can also understand why He is coming back to judge the earth. I have merged the final aspect of Jesus' eyes of fire with the description of His feet. The word translated "fine brass" is a unique compound word that is not clear in its meaning. However, multiple commentators say it probably refers to brass that is white-hot in the furnace. It most definitely points us to the altar where the judgment for sin was paid with the shedding of blood.

Jesus' fiery, passionate love for us caused Him to willingly be the sacrificial lamb slain to suffer judgment for our sins.

> Surely He has borne our griefs and carried our sorrows; yet we esteemed Him stricken, smitten by God, and afflicted. But He was wounded for our transgressions, He was bruised for our iniquities; the chastisement for our peace was upon Him, and by His stripes we are healed.
> —ISAIAH 53:4–5

The eyes of fire and feet of brass also reveal to us that God is going to come back to remove everything that hinders love. Wickedness, rebellion, perversion, selfishness, pride, and all manner of evil shall be removed from the earth. Both images— eyes of fire and feet of brass—are of flaming-hot, all-consuming fire that purifies.

An end-time prophecy from Isaiah 66 speaks of the day of the Lord.

> For behold, the LORD will come with fire and with His
> chariots, like a whirlwind, to render His anger with fury,
> and His rebuke with flames of fire. For by fire and by His
> sword the LORD will judge all flesh; and the slain of the
> LORD shall be many.
>
> —ISAIAH 66:15–16

Put this deep in your spirit. The reason God hates sin so much is because it causes us to be separated from His eternal purpose for us, to be the bride of Christ. Sin makes it impossible for us to coexist in oneness with God, which is why we were created.

It has become popular today to teach that God does not judge anymore. This is a grave mistake and completely unscriptural. The judgment of God is released to remove the ravages of sin. Sin destroys because it spreads like a cancer through everything it touches. The only way for sin to be removed is to destroy it. Sin must be put to death. "For the wages of sin is death" (Rom. 6:23).

God, in His love, must finally put an end to sin to fully save and spare His bride. We who are born again are forgiven, but we still suffer from the ravages of sin and its effects upon humanity. Jesus is coming back to the earth to rule and reign here. His love for His bride requires Him to finally judge all sin in those who have not repented and ultimately cast them into the lake of fire.

When Jesus executes His final judgments on the earth, the bride (the church, Christians) will proclaim that He is righteous and just to have judged and poured out His wrath. The bride will understand that His fierce, fiery judgments were sent to remove everything that hindered love.

> After these things I heard a loud voice of a great multi-
> tude in heaven, saying, "Alleluia! Salvation and glory and
> honor and power belong to the Lord our God! For true
> and righteous are His judgments, because He has judged
> the great harlot who corrupted the earth with her forni-
> cation; and He has avenged on her the blood of His ser-
> vants shed by her."
>
> —REVELATION 19:1–2

In verse 2, who declares that "true and righteous are His judgments"? The bride of Christ. "Let us be glad and rejoice and give Him glory, for the marriage of the Lamb has come, and His wife has made herself ready" (Rev. 19:7, MEV). The bride of Christ is the one who makes the declaration about the judgments. We will rejoice when we see that "the Lord has washed away the filth of the daughters of Zion and has purged the blood of Jerusalem from the midst by the spirit of justice and by the spirit of burning" (Isa. 4:4, MEV).

The concept that judgment is contrary to the nature of Jesus is false. Love demands justice, which produces judgment. The purpose of judgment is to remove sin, either by leading people to repentance or by removing the rebellious ones permanently.

Jesus' fiery eyes bring judgment in three areas: (1) the judgment of the ungodly, (2) the judgment exercised by the church among the brethren, and (3) the judgment that God allows in the lives of saints to remove rebellion from their hearts.

1. First will be judgment of the ungodly.

> But the heavens and the earth which are now preserved by the same word, are reserved for fire until the day of judgment and perdition of ungodly men....But the day of the Lord will come as a thief in the night, in which the heavens will pass away with a great noise, and the elements will melt with fervent heat; both the earth and the works that are in it will be burned up. Therefore, since all these things will be dissolved, what manner of persons ought you to be in holy conduct and godliness, looking for and hastening the coming of the day of God, because of which the heavens will be dissolved, being on fire, and the elements will melt with fervent heat?
>
> —2 PETER 3:7, 10–12

Peter says that this revelation of the fiery judgment of God should cause us to live godly lives. The false teaching that has spread through the hyper-grace message, which says that we do not have to live godly lives, is contrary to Scripture.

This judgment of the ungodly is not reserved exclusively for the return of Christ. God has and will intervene in the affairs of men to stop wickedness from spreading too far. He has restrained wickedness through judgment throughout human history and will continue to do so until the end. There will be a season called the great tribulation when God will allow wickedness to run rampant, but even then He will send judgments, one after another, to give people one final time to repent while they are alive.

In the last days, multitudes will repent and come to the saving knowledge of Jesus.

> After these things I looked, and behold, a great multitude which no one could number, of all nations, tribes, peoples, and tongues, standing before the throne and before the Lamb...."Who are these arrayed in white robes, and where did they come from?"..."These are the ones who come out of the great tribulation, and washed their robes and made them white in the blood of the Lamb."
> —REVELATION 7:9, 13–14

Multitudes will double down on their wickedness in the face of God's judgments.

> But the rest of mankind, who were not killed by these plagues, did not repent of the works of their hands.
> —REVELATION 9:20

2. Next, the church will exercise judgment among the brethren. When Ananias and Sapphira sinned by lying to the Holy Spirit and the apostles, God sent judgment. In the face of such incredible glory manifested in those days, this act of selfishness, pride, and deception would have spread like a ravenous cancer and damaged the early church. God could not allow this sin, so He judged them severely.

When a man in Corinth was having a sexual relationship with the woman who was his father's wife, God through Paul ordered the church to expel this man. Paul said to turn him over to the devil. "In the name of our Lord Jesus Christ, when you are assembled, along with my spirit, in the power of our Lord Jesus Christ, deliver him to Satan for the destruction of the flesh, so that the spirit may be saved on the day of the Lord Jesus" (1 Cor. 5:4–5, MEV). This judgment was not immediate death but was Jesus, through the church, exercising the power of God and turning the sinful brother over to destruction. The hope was that he would repent and ultimately be saved.

The church was aware of the man's sin, but they were "arrogant." Their pride in their gifts and "wisdom" caused them to fail to deal with the sin in the camp. Maybe they viewed themselves as loving and compassionate, or they looked at the blessings they had and figured God didn't mind. Paul told them, "Your boasting is not good. Do you not know that a little yeast leavens the whole batch?" (1 Cor. 5:6, MEV).

Because sin spreads and perverts everything it touches, God requires the church to deal with those who brazenly and willfully continue in their sin. I do not believe this is talking about those who are genuinely struggling with sin, even addictions. The previous examples are people, members of the church, who in the face of such outpourings of God's glory and power rebelled against God's Word and brought great danger to the other saints.

I have helped many people who have been bound by sin and have struggled for a long time. However, when a person, in the face of the clarity of God's Word and the power of the Holy Spirit, rejects the call to holiness and continues to live a sin-filled life, God requires judgment. The judgment may be death, it may be removal from the church, or it may even be weakness and sickness as in 1 Corinthians 11:29–32:

> For he who eats and drinks in an unworthy manner eats and drinks judgment to himself, not discerning the Lord's body. For this reason many are weak and sick among you, and many sleep. For if we would judge ourselves, we would not be judged. But when we are judged, we are chastened by the Lord, that we may not be condemned with the world.

This verse leads us into the third area.

3. God will allow judgment in the lives of saints to remove rebellion from their hearts. In studying God's Word, context is everything. The revelation of Jesus with eyes of fire and feet of brass is given directly before He rebukes the church of Thyatira and warns them of impending judgment if they do not change.

> And to the angel of the church in Thyatira write, "These things says the Son of God, who has eyes like a flame of fire, and His feet like fine brass....'Nevertheless I have a few things against you, because you allow that woman Jezebel, who calls herself a prophetess, to teach and seduce My servants to commit sexual immorality and eat things sacrificed to idols. And I gave her time to repent of her sexual immorality, and she did not repent. Indeed I will cast her into a sickbed, and those who commit adultery with her into great tribulation, unless they repent of their deeds. I will kill her children with death, and all the churches shall know that I am He who searches the minds and hearts. And I will give to each one of you according to your works.'"
>
> —REVELATION 2:18, 20–23

This church, like so many of our modern churches, allowed a teaching that said committing sexual immorality and idolatry was not a problem. Basically, she was teaching the modern version of the grace message. Jesus rebuked this church and declared the judgment that was coming to her and those who embraced her false teaching. He gave her time to repent, as He does with all of us, but she would not, so He sent judgment. These are Christians that He is judging.

> For if we sin willfully after we have received the knowledge of the truth, there no longer remains a sacrifice for sins, but a certain fearful expectation of judgment, and fiery indignation which will devour the adversaries.
>
> —HEBREWS 10:26–27

The fiery, jealous desire for you in Jesus' eyes is so strong that He will deal with your unrepentant sin if that's what it takes to make you holy. "For whom the Lord loves He disciplines, and scourges every son whom He receives" (Heb. 12:6, MEV). His love is what motivates His judgment. He is so jealous for every part of your heart and affections that He will, through long-suffering, allow judgment, if needed, to cause you to finally surrender those areas to Him. He will judge the ungodly to slow and eventually remove the sin that destroys His eternal plan in people's lives and injures His bride.

Jesus' judgments are not given because He is mean, spiteful, unkind, and unloving. It is because He is filled with eyes of fiery, passionate desire for His bride. For this reason, He will remove everything that hinders His love. He will burn out of us all that stands between us and Him, and He will burn out of the earth everything that rejects His amazing love.

> John answered, saying to all, "I indeed baptize you with water; but One mightier than I is coming, whose sandal strap I am not worthy to loose. *He will baptize you with the Holy Spirit and fire.* His winnowing fan is in His hand, and He will thoroughly clean out His threshing floor, and gather the wheat into His barn; but the chaff He will burn with *unquenchable fire.*"
> —LUKE 3:16–17, EMPHASIS ADDED

Prayer

Father, pierce me with Your eyes of fire. Show me where I must repent, and remove anything that hinders Your love. Purify my heart, my mind, and my soul so I may always be close to You. Keep Your eyes of fiery passion fixed on me so I may never be separated from You. In Jesus' holy name, amen.

Day 24
A VOICE LIKE MANY WATERS, PART 1

His voice as the sound of many waters...
—Revelation 1:15

T HIS IS ONE of my favorite descriptions of Jesus because it reveals to us not only His nature but also how we are in full partnership with Him in releasing the glory of God and the end-time events into the earth.

This description of His voice speaks to us of God's last-days manifestation, and of a prophetic prayer and worship movement that will result in the greatest demonstration of the power and glory of God that the world has ever seen.

The first place this phrase is used is in the Book of Ezekiel.

> When they went, I heard the noise of their wings, like the noise of many waters, like the voice of the Almighty, a tumult like the noise of an army; and when they stood still, they let down their wings.
>
> —EZEKIEL 1:24

> Afterward he brought me to the gate, the gate that faces toward the east. And behold, the glory of the God of Israel came from the way of the east. His voice was like the sound of many waters; and the earth shone with His glory.
>
> —EZEKIEL 43:1–2

Both of these times we see Jesus' voice being described as the sound or noise of many waters. We also see a similar description in Daniel 10 that very closely matches John's vision in Revelation 1.

> His body was like beryl, his face like the appearance of lightning, his eyes like torches of fire, his arms and feet like burnished bronze in color, and the sound of his words like the voice of a multitude.
>
> —DANIEL 10:6

And once more we see it in Revelation 14:2: "And I heard a sound from heaven, like the sound of many waters and like the sound of a great thunder. I heard the sound of harpists playing their harps" (MEV).

As we study God's Word, we look for things that are associated with these descriptions to help us gain understanding. We see several things associated with the sound of many waters. We see the living creatures who minister at the throne of God. We see it as the sound of an army. We see the glory of God being manifested in the earth. We see the sound of harpists playing their harps.

First, I want us to look at the living creatures and the harps. The living creatures, which are later identified as cherubim, are heavenly beings that worship before the throne of God day and night. "The four living creatures had six wings each, and they were covered with eyes all around. All day and night, without ceasing, they were saying: 'Holy, holy, holy, Lord God Almighty, who was, and is, and is to come'" (Rev. 4:8, MEV).

Some debate whether these are the exact same creatures because Ezekiel's creatures had four wings and the Revelation creatures had six wings, but otherwise they seem the same. Either way all these creatures are at the throne of God, in the midst of the glory of God, worshipping and ministering to God day and night. Their wings produce a sound that is like the voice of the Almighty.

We also see these creatures with harps and bowls. "When He had taken the scroll, the four living creatures and the twenty-four elders fell down before the Lamb, each one having a harp, and golden bowls full of incense, which are the prayers of saints. And they sang a new song" (Rev. 5:8–9, MEV).

Our attention then must be drawn to the harps, which we will see in a moment are always connected to the prophetic, and the bowls filled with incense, which are the prayers of the saints.

> "But now bring me a harpist." While the harpist was playing, the hand of the LORD came on Elisha and he said, "This is what the LORD says: I will fill this valley with pools of water."
>
> —2 KINGS 3:15–16, NIV

When God called Saul to be king, Saul had an encounter with this prophetic music. We often see a correlation between the playing of music/minstrels and the release of the prophetic.

> After that you shall come to the hill of God where the Philistine garrison is. And it will happen, when you have come there to the city, that you will meet a group of prophets coming down from the high place with a stringed instrument, a tambourine, a flute, and a harp before them; and they will be prophesying. Then the Spirit of the LORD will come upon you, and you will prophesy with them and be turned into another man.
>
> —1 SAMUEL 10:5–6

King David understood the connection between music and the prophetic. "Moreover David and the captains of the army separated for the service some of the sons of Asaph, of Heman, and of Jeduthun, who should prophesy with harps, stringed instruments, and cymbals...who prophesied with a harp to give thanks and to praise the LORD" (1 Chron. 25:1, 3).

The harps are connected to the kind of worship that releases the prophetic word of the Lord. Jesus' voice, the sound of many waters, is directly connected to prophetic worship and prayer.

Look at how the Amplified Bible, Classic Edition translates Revelation 14:2:

> And I heard a voice from heaven like the sound of great waters and like the rumbling of mighty thunder; the voice I heard [seemed like the music] of harpists accompanying themselves on their harps.

It says the voice of Jesus seemed like the music of a harpist. It is interesting to note that many of the Jewish prayers are sung. God's people have always had a musical union with the prophetic and with prayer.

So why is this important? These descriptions in Revelation are to prepare an end-time people to face the most intense season the world will ever see. Through the description of His voice as the sound of many waters, Jesus is revealing to us that a new dimension of a prophetic prayer and worship movement will be released in the last days.

This is what Joel was referring to when he said, "And it shall come to pass afterward that I will pour out My Spirit on all flesh; your sons and your daughters shall prophesy, your old men shall dream dreams, your young men shall see visions. And also on My menservants and on My maidservants I will pour out My Spirit in those days. And I will show wonders in the heavens and in the earth: blood and fire and pillars of smoke. The sun shall be turned into darkness, and the moon into blood, before the coming of the great and awesome day of the LORD" (Joel 2:28–31).

This prophetic manifestation of the revelation of Jesus through worship and prayer will cause the greatest release of the glory of God upon the earth that we have ever seen. As we see Him, we will become more like Him. Our hearts, our thoughts, our words, and our actions will be in line with His to the point that we will sound like Jesus. The bride will be so in tune with Jesus that our prophetic worship and prayers will sound like Jesus Himself.

> And I heard, as it were, the voice of a great multitude, *as the sound of many waters* and as the sound of mighty thunderings, saying, "Alleluia! For the Lord God Omnipotent reigns! Let us be glad and rejoice and give

Him glory, for the marriage of the Lamb has come, and
His wife has made herself ready."
—REVELATION 19:6–7, EMPHASIS ADDED

Jesus' voice was described in Revelation 14:2 "like the voice
of many waters, and like the voice of loud thunder." Then, in
Revelation 19, the bride's voice is described the same. The worship and prayer anointing in the last days will be filled with the
revelation of Jesus, who He is and what He is focused on. Unlike
a lot of what we see today, where the focus is on who we are and
what we like, this prophetic prayer and worship movement will be
all about Jesus.

There are pockets of this end-time prophetic prayer and worship movement throughout the world, but Satan is trying to abort
it. Just as Lucifer did in heaven, Satan wants to redirect the worship away from God and onto another. The spirit of the Antichrist
will always try to make everything about me, myself, and I.

I will ascend into heaven, I will exalt my throne above the
stars of God; I will also sit on the mount of the congrega-
tion on the farthest sides of the north; I will ascend above
the heights of the clouds, I will be like the Most High.
—ISAIAH 14:13–14

The enemy tries to pervert this prophetic worship and prayer
movement by getting us to make it all about ourselves. The shift is
subtle but very significant. The strategy of the enemy has always
been to take our focus off God, His glory, and His commands and
focus on ourselves instead.

In the Garden of Eden the serpent convinced Eve to rebel by
getting her to focus on what she thought would benefit herself.
"When the woman saw that the tree was good for food, that it was
pleasing to the eyes and a tree desirable to make one wise, she took
of its fruit and ate; and she gave to her husband with her, and he
ate" (Gen. 3:6, MEV).

As we see in the perversion of much of the teaching today, the enemy has convinced us that the commands of God for a holy life are hindering us from experiencing freedom and fulfillment. This worldly and ungodly philosophy is expressed in one of Disney's most famous songs that so many Christians sing with their children: "Let It Go." The most demonic line in the song is when the character says there is no right or wrong and no rules for her—she's free. Very few modern Christians realize that this line is all about throwing off the commands of morality and doing what makes you feel good.

This is the end-time demonic mindset that this prophetic worship and prayer movement will be pushing back against. The prophetic prayer and worship movement will be manifested in the face of the world doing all it can to throw off the "restraints" of biblical morality and teachings.

Psalm 2 is an end-time prophetic message.

> Why do the nations rage, and the people plot a vain thing? The kings of the earth set themselves, and the rulers take counsel together, against the LORD and against His Anointed, saying, "Let us break Their bonds in pieces and cast away Their cords from us."
>
> —PSALM 2:1–3

The time has come when the nations and world influencers will collectively cast God and His Word out of all influence in society. The Word of God and His demands for holiness are increasingly being demonized and called evil. We see this already happening with the radical homosexual agenda, transgender ideology, and socialist indoctrinations.

In the midst of this increased darkness being released upon the earth caused by this rejection of God and His Word, God will send the greatest manifestation and revelation of His Son Jesus. The voice with the sound of many waters will be heard throughout the world and cause the glory of God to be seen upon His people.

Arise, shine; for your light has come! And the glory of the
LORD is risen upon you. For behold, the darkness shall
cover the earth, and deep darkness the people; but the
LORD will arise over you, and His glory will be seen upon
you. The Gentiles shall come to your light, and kings to
the brightness of your rising.

—Isaiah 60:1–3

We saw this glory coming into the earth in Ezekiel 43:2: "And
behold, the glory of the God of Israel came from the way of the
east. His voice was like the sound of many waters; and the earth
shone with His glory."

The voice of Jesus through the prophetic prayer and worship
movement will release a manifestation and demonstration of the
glory of God like the world has never seen.

Prayer

*Father, thank You for preparing Your bride for the
greatest manifestation of Your power and glory
the world has ever seen. Give me the revelation I
need to help release this end-time prayer and worship movement. Anoint me with the wisdom and
discernment needed to keep the focus on You and
off me. Make Your voice of many waters heard, and
cause Your glory to shine all around. In Jesus' holy
name, amen.*

Day 25
A VOICE LIKE MANY WATERS, PART 2

And I heard, as it were, the voice of a great multitude, as the sound of many waters and as the sound of mighty thunderings, saying, "Alleluia! For the Lord God Omnipotent reigns!"
—REVELATION 19:6

WHEN WE BEHOLD Jesus as He is, we will be filled with the knowledge of His plans and purposes. We will declare the glorious beauty of His holiness as we are drawn up into the heavenlies to see Him with prophetic eyes. A greater authority will come upon us, and we will move under a new prophetic prayer and worship anointing. We will pray what He prays, and we will say and sing what He says.

The focus will be on Him, not predominately us. We will say, "He must increase, but I must decrease. He who comes from above is above all" (John 3:30–31, MEV). When we see Him, we will declare through prayer and song what is declared at the throne of God. These prophetic declarations will be mixed with the fire from the altar of heaven and will release the last-days events into the earth.

> Then another angel, having a golden censer, came and stood at the altar. He was given much incense, that he should offer it with the prayers of all the saints upon the golden altar which was before the throne. And the smoke of the incense, with the prayers of the saints, ascended before God from the angel's hand. Then the angel took the censer, filled it with fire from the altar, and threw it to the earth. And there were noises, thunderings, lightnings, and an earthquake. So the seven angels who had the seven trumpets prepared themselves to sound.
> —REVELATION 8:3–6

When the prayers of the saints ascend before God and mix with the fire from the altar, the seven angels release their judgments upon the earth.

We see this same manifestation of noises, thunderings, lightnings, and an earthquake in Revelation 11:19: "Then the temple of God was opened in heaven, and the ark of His covenant was seen in His temple. And there were lightnings, noises, thunderings, an earthquake, and great hail." This verse follows soon after another prophetic declaration of what will happen in heaven.

> Then the seventh angel sounded: And there were loud voices in heaven, saying, "The kingdoms of this world have become the kingdoms of our Lord and of His Christ, and He shall reign forever and ever!"
>
> —REVELATION 11:15

We see the prophetic prayers of the saints rise before the throne of God, where they are mixed with fire from the altar and thrown back to the earth, which symbolizes God answering those prophetic prayers. We then see the events of the seventh trumpet—the completion of the judgments of God upon the earth to bring men to repentance before the seven bowls of wrath are poured out.

Our loud voices in heaven, through prophetic prayer and worship, will release the final manifestation of the glory of God and the judgments of God upon the earth. "And I heard, as it were, the voice of a great multitude, as the sound of many waters and as the sound of mighty thunderings, saying, 'Alleluia! For the Lord God Omnipotent reigns!'" (Rev. 19:6).

We are Jesus' prayer partners. We declare who He is and His righteous judgments. Jesus said, "As the Father has sent Me, I also send you" (John 20:21). "The words that I speak to you I do not speak on My own authority; but the Father who dwells in Me does the works" (John 14:10). "Most assuredly, I say to you, the Son can do nothing of Himself, but what He sees the Father do; for whatever He does, the Son also does in like manner. For the Father loves the Son, and shows Him all things that He Himself does;

and He will show Him greater works than these, that you may marvel" (John 5:19–20). "I do nothing of Myself; but as My Father taught Me, I speak these things. And He who sent Me is with Me. The Father has not left Me alone, for I always do those things that please Him" (John 8:28–29). "For I have not spoken on My own authority; but the Father who sent Me gave Me a command, what I should say and what I should speak" (John 12:49).

I want to exhort you to be like Jesus. He did everything according to what He heard His Father say and do. As the Father sent Jesus to earth, so He sends us. We are to prophetically pray, declare, and sing what Jesus did.

The Holy Spirit will give you prophetic revelation. He "will guide you into all truth; for He will not speak on His own authority, but whatever He hears He will speak; and He will tell you things to come. He will glorify Me, for He will take of what is Mine and declare it to you" (John 16:13–14). "Most assuredly, I say to you, he who believes in Me, the works that I do he will do also; and greater works than these he will do, because I go to My Father. And whatever you ask in My name, that I will do, that the Father may be glorified in the Son. If you ask anything in My name, I will do it" (John 14:12–14).

In this vision we see John being invited by Jesus to the throne of God. "After these things I looked, and behold, a door standing open in heaven. And the first voice which I heard was like a trumpet speaking with me, saying, 'Come up here, and I will show you things which must take place after this'" (Rev. 4:1).

I believe this invitation was an insight into the plans of God in revealing Himself and His workings in the last days at a new and unprecedented level. Jesus' voice, like a trumpet, says, "Come up here, and I will show you things that must take place after this."

In the age called "the maturity of the times and the climax of the ages" (Eph. 1:10, AMPC), God is going to make "known to us the mystery (secret) of His will (of His plan, of His purpose)" (Eph. 1:9, AMPC). As He brings us into this experience, Jesus gives us a command in the voice that sounds like many waters. He tells us, "Therefore do not fear them. For there is nothing covered that will not be revealed, and hidden that will not be known. Whatever I tell you in the dark, speak in the light; and what you hear in the ear, preach on the housetops" (Matt. 10:26–27). In other words, when He reveals something to us, we are to prophesy it, sing it, preach it, tell it, and pray it.

This prophetic worship and prayer anointing will bind demonic strongholds and release the written judgments upon the ungodly leaders. This will include prophetic singing. Psalm 149 gives us powerful insight into this reality.

> Praise the LORD! Sing to the LORD a new song, and His praise in the assembly of saints....Let the saints be joyful in glory; let them sing aloud on their beds. Let the high praises of God be in their mouth, and a two-edged sword in their hand, to execute vengeance on the nations, and punishments on the peoples; to bind their kings with chains, and their nobles with fetters of iron; to execute on them the written judgment—this honor have all His saints. Praise the LORD!
>
> —PSALM 149:1, 5–9

David declares, "He has put a new song in my mouth—praise to our God; many will see it and fear, and will trust in the LORD" (Ps. 40:3).

Two manifestations happen when this new prophetic song flows. Many will gain the fear of God, and many will trust in the Lord. The same manifestation of the voice of the sound of many waters will release the fear of God and cause many to turn to God.

Another one of David's end-time prophecies is found in Psalm 98.

> Oh, sing to the LORD a new song! For He has done marvelous things; His right hand and His holy arm have gained Him the victory. The LORD has made known His salvation; His righteousness He has revealed in the sight of the nations. He has remembered His mercy and His faithfulness to the house of Israel; all the ends of the earth have seen the salvation of our God.
>
> —PSALM 98:1–3

When we sing new prophetic songs, God's glory will manifest in the earth and His judgments will be released. "For He is coming to judge the earth. With righteousness He shall judge the world, and the peoples with equity" (Ps. 98:9).

And finally we will end with Psalm 96.

> Oh, sing to the LORD a new song! Sing to the LORD, all the earth. Sing to the LORD, bless His name; proclaim the good news of His salvation from day to day. Declare His glory among the nations, His wonders among all peoples. For the LORD is great and greatly to be praised; He is to be feared above all gods....Oh, worship the LORD in the beauty of holiness! Tremble before Him, all the earth.... For He is coming, for He is coming to judge the earth. He shall judge the world with righteousness, and the peoples with His truth.
>
> —PSALM 96:1–4, 9, 13

We will see the greatest manifestation of the revelation of Jesus of any generation. This manifestation will come to the church on an unprecedented level. We will flow in a last-days prophetic prayer and worship anointing that will result in the greatest harvest of souls the world has ever seen, and it will release the end-time judgments of God upon the ungodly. This honor will belong to all the saints.

Prayer

Father, fill me with the knowledge of Your plans and purposes. Put Your words on my lips, and fill me with new songs as I flow in prophetic prayer and worship. Bind all demonic strongholds and release Your judgments upon them. In Jesus' holy name, amen.

Day 26
LEADERS OF THE CHURCH

The mystery of the seven stars which you saw in My
right hand, and the seven golden lampstands: The seven
stars are the angels of the seven churches, and the seven
lampstands which you saw are the seven churches.

—REVELATION 1:20

STARS ARE LOFTY and heavenly. They represent something
from the heavenly realm. These angels are the men who are
the leaders of these churches. It is clear they are not literal angels
because in each of the messages to the seven churches, many of
which are rebukes, Jesus says, "To the angel of the church of..."
The word *angel* here means messenger, and it speaks of God's
appointed fivefold ministers.

There is a very important truth we all must embrace if we are
going to fully mature into our God-given destinies. Jesus—not
man—anoints and appoints His leaders within His church, and
He calls them His angels. In the Book of Revelation, Jesus states
that they have a special calling and access to minister to Him and
to His people on His behalf.

Jesus says these leaders are His and He has them in His right
hand. The right hand always speaks of God's strength, salvation,
and deliverance. He will use these leaders to exercise His strength,
salvation, deliverance, and victory in the earth.

The church is Jesus' structure for His body to grow, and the
stars are Jesus' leaders. We need to learn how to properly relate
to both. When we see Jesus with the stars in His hand, we see not
only that He anointed and appointed His leaders but also that He
holds them accountable. We see this in the rebukes to the "angels"
of five of the seven churches.

To properly grow and mature, we must learn to fully trust Jesus'
leadership. Jesus is not telling you to trust His leaders; He is telling

you to trust Him. The reason so many people have issues with trusting church leaders is because they have issues with trusting Jesus.

Do we really believe that Jesus has the leaders in His hand? Do we really believe that He is capable of directing, instructing, using, and dealing with human vessels?

God never asked us to trust one another. He commanded us to love one another. If we are to live in the revelation of who He is, we will have to rise to a new level of trusting Him.

Maybe you say, "Well, I trust God, but I don't trust church leaders." Jesus would say, "Then are you really trusting Me?" The Book of Proverbs teaches us the process of trusting His leadership.

> Trust in the LORD with all your heart, and lean not on your own understanding; in all your ways acknowledge Him, and He shall direct your paths.
>
> —PROVERBS 3:5–6

Let's examine these Scripture verses in detail.

"Trust in the Lord." You must "trust, rely on, put confidence in" the Lord.[1] Trusting is putting your full confidence in Jesus. You are relying on His character, His nature, His authority, and His ability to fulfill His plans and purposes.

"...with all your heart." The heart is "the locus of a person's thoughts (mind), volition (their will), emotions."[2] You must trust Jesus' leadership with all your emotions, your will, and your thoughts.

"And lean not on your own understanding." The sense of the word *lean* is to put trust and confidence in something. The verse says do not put any trust or confidence in your own understanding. This is incredibly important because this is where the church falls apart.

Instead of trusting and putting confidence in Jesus, we rely upon our feelings, our perceptions, and our ideas. We lean upon our preferred methods, ideas, and feelings, and we question God's leaders because we would do things differently. We allow the noise of opinions and gossip to cause us to stop trusting in God.

"In all your ways acknowledge Him." The sense of the word *acknowledge* is *to accept someone to be what is claimed.* In the context of the stars in Jesus' hand it means to accept that He has the character, authority, and perfect nature to lead, guide, and correct His appointed leaders.

The phrase "in all your ways" means to "behave in a particular way, in the manner one conducts one's life."[3] In all the ways you conduct your life, know the character and nature of Jesus. Act like He is who He claims to be, the One who holds the stars in His hand.

"And He shall direct your paths." The promise from these verses is He shall direct, that is, "make linear movement with... no wandering or turning from a course, implying movement with purpose or ease," [4] your path, which means "a way of life, destiny in a life."[5]

If you trust in Jesus' character and nature with all your thoughts, will, and emotions—not your feelings and perceptions—He will make your life a straight path and not allow anything or anyone to cause you to wander or turn you from your destiny.

Jesus is saying, "Fully trust Me and My leadership. I am in control. I have anointed and appointed My leaders, and I know how to use them to fulfill My purposes in your life." If you lean upon your understanding, feelings, emotions, and so on, the implication here is you will wander and be turned from your course.

These seven stars in Jesus' right hand are gifts from Him to us, to impart revelation knowledge so we can grow in grace. He has given them to us to teach, lead, guide, correct, and empower us to fulfill our destinies. When we receive from these gifts He has placed inside the stars in His hand, we can access greater power, wisdom, strength, and revelation knowledge of Jesus.

This image of the stars in Jesus' hand also sends a fearful warning to those who are leaders that they are His representatives and will be held to a much higher standard. To the leaders Jesus says the following:

- **They are My flock, not yours.** "Therefore take heed to yourselves and to all the flock, among which the Holy Spirit has made you overseers, to shepherd the church of God which He purchased with His own blood" (Acts 20:28).

- **You must live holy and above reproach.** "It is an abomination for kings to commit wickedness, for a throne is established by righteousness" (Prov. 16:12).

- **Your teaching and example must lead people in the ways of righteousness.** "Whoever causes one of these little ones who believe in Me to sin, it would be better for him if a millstone were hung around his neck, and he were drowned in the depth of the sea" (Matt. 18:6).

- **You will be held to a much higher standard.** "Not many [of you] should become teachers [serving in an official teaching capacity], my brothers and sisters, for you know that we [who are teachers] will be judged by a higher standard [because we have assumed greater accountability and more condemnation if we teach incorrectly]" (Jas. 3:1, AMP).

- **You must cause the people to revere and honor Jesus by how you minister to and for Him.** "By those who come near Me I must be regarded as holy; and before all the people..." (Lev. 10:3).

- **Glorify Jesus in all you do.** "I must be glorified" (Lev. 10:3).

- **Teach the people that Jesus must be treated with the highest honor.** "The priests shall teach My people the difference between the holy and

the common or profane, and cause them to dis-
tinguish between the unclean and the clean"
(Ezek. 44:23, AMPC).

Jesus holds the stars, His leaders, in His right hand. He has
exalted them, and He will hold them accountable. The stars,
leaders, must see themselves in Jesus' right hand and tremble at
His word. It is a fearful thing to fail to represent Jesus correctly.

> Therefore, you shepherds, hear the word of the LORD:
> "As I live," says the Lord GOD, "surely because My flock
> became a prey, and My flock became food for every
> beast of the field, because there was no shepherd, nor
> did My shepherds search for My flock, but the shep-
> herds fed themselves and did not feed My flock"—there-
> fore, O shepherds, hear the word of the LORD! Thus says
> the Lord GOD: "Behold, I am against the shepherds, and
> I will require My flock at their hand; I will cause them
> to cease feeding the sheep, and the shepherds shall feed
> themselves no more; for I will deliver My flock from their
> mouths, that they may no longer be food for them."
> —EZEKIEL 34:7–10

JESUS USES HIS STARS IN THE MIDST OF HIS LAMPSTANDS

Jesus created the local church, as we learned in the seven golden
lampstands teaching, to reveal and manifest Himself in the earth.
Jesus is the head of His body, the church. The stars are Jesus'
anointed and appointed leaders to administrate His kingdom
authority. These stars, His leaders, are His delegated representatives given the responsibility to care for, nurture, lead, guide, correct, and teach His people.

When we try to grow in the revelation of Jesus and yet have an
improper relationship with His church and/or His leaders, we are
destined for weakness. You cannot separate Jesus from His church
and His leaders. What you honor is drawn toward you, and what

you dishonor will go from you. If you fail to honor the gifts, the "stars" of God, you will lose what they have for you.

God anoints and appoints leaders, fivefold ministers, to release revelation gifts to mature and empower the entire body of Christ. Without these leaders functioning properly, the church cannot fully mature.

One of the reasons so much of the church is tossed back and forth by every wind of doctrine is because we have lost the revelation of the stars in Jesus' hand. When the saints function under the revelation gifts that flow through the fivefold ministry, the body of Christ will grow and mature. Speaking about this process, Paul says this about the church:

> [That it might develop] until we all attain oneness in the faith and in the comprehension of the [full and accurate] knowledge of the Son of God, that [we might arrive] at really mature manhood (the completeness of personality which is nothing less than the standard height of Christ's own perfection), the measure of the stature of the fullness of the Christ and the completeness found in Him.
>
> —EPHESIANS 4:13, AMPC

Since Jesus calls His leaders angels and refers to them as stars, we need to see them as Jesus sees them. Let us not be as the culture of our day, which replaces honor with scorn, criticism, and mocking. We gossip, complain, accuse, and belittle leaders we don't like. This is wrong. We must honor and uphold them. The culture of honor is the culture of the kingdom of heaven. David honored King Saul even while being pursued by him. Daniel honored King Nebuchadnezzar even when he was a captive. Paul taught us to "honor your father and mother...that it may be well with you and you may live long on the earth" (Eph. 6:2–3, MEV).

Honor is mentioned throughout Scripture. "You shall rise before a gray head, and honor the face of an old man, and fear your God: I am the LORD" (Lev. 19:32, MEV).

When you honor, it opens your heart to receive. When you dishonor, your heart closes.

> Let the elders who rule well be counted worthy of double
> honor, especially those who labor in the word and doc-
> trine. For the Scripture says, "You shall not muzzle an ox
> while it treads out the grain," and, "The laborer is worthy
> of his wages."
>
> —1 TIMOTHY 5:17–18

How we treat God's church—the lampstands—and God's
stars—His leaders—is how we treat Him. "He who receives you
receives Me, and he who receives Me receives Him who sent me.
He who receives a prophet in the name of a prophet shall receive a
prophet's reward" (Matt. 10:40–41, MEV).

God says, "For those who honor Me, I will honor, and those
that despise Me will be humbled" (1 Sam. 2:30, MEV).

Jesus takes how we treat His chosen leaders very seriously and
personally. I am well aware that not everyone who carries the title
of apostle, prophet, evangelist, pastor, or teacher in the church is
anointed and appointed by God. I am writing only of those He
has chosen. We must discern those whom God has chosen in the
church and treat them accordingly. Paul said to the Galatians,
"You...received me as an angel of God, even as Christ Jesus" (Gal.
4:14, MEV).

The stars in Jesus' hand are His. He holds them and gives them
power and authority for His divine purposes. Honor them as you
would honor Him because they are the leaders He anointed and
appointed.

Prayer

Father, I put my full trust in You. You have anointed and appointed Your leaders in Your body to help me grow into the full and accurate knowledge of Jesus. Jesus, I choose to trust in Your leadership. I pray for Your grace and mercy to be upon Your appointed leaders. Strengthen them, lead them, guide them, correct them, and use them for Your kingdom. Bring me to Your appointed leaders and help me to have a proper relationship with them. In Jesus' holy name, amen.

Day 27
GOD'S WORD IS A SWORD, PART 1

Out of His mouth went a sharp two-edged sword.
—REVELATION 1:16

THE WORD *SWORD* in the Greek language means two-edged, sharp. In fact, the word *sword* here is specific to a broadsword called a *rhomphaia*, which was "strictly a large Thracian broadsword."[1] This kind of sword was a powerful weapon that could be used for thrusting, swiping, and chopping. It was a powerful weapon believed to be the same type used by Goliath.

Some preachers have said that the two-edged sword has one side that cuts and another side that heals. However, it is very unlikely that is the image John saw. John would have been familiar with the rhomphaia, a powerful weapon of war. When we see this sword coming out of Jesus' mouth, we must see His Word as a weapon that can penetrate, expose, judge, and overpower.

> For the Word that God speaks is alive and full of power [making it active, operative, energizing, and effective]; it is sharper than any two-edged sword, penetrating to the dividing line of the breath of life (soul) and [the immortal] spirit, and of joints and marrow [of the deepest parts of our nature], exposing and sifting and analyzing and judging the very thoughts and purposes of the heart. And not a creature exists that is concealed from His sight, but all things are open and exposed, naked and defenseless to the eyes of Him with Whom we have to do.
> —HEBREWS 4:12–13, AMPC

The words of Jesus are alive. "It is the Spirit who gives life. The flesh profits nothing. The words that I speak to you are spirit and are life" (John 6:63, MEV). Peter then declared, "Lord, to whom shall we go? You have the words of eternal life" (John 6:68, MEV).

> Most assuredly, I say to you, he who hears My word and believes in Him who sent Me has everlasting life, and shall not come into judgment, but has passed from death into life.
>
> —JOHN 5:24

The words of Jesus are active and operating continually.

> So shall My word be that goes forth from My mouth; it shall not return to Me void, but it shall accomplish what I please, and it shall prosper in the thing for which I sent it.
>
> —ISAIAH 55:11

> Heaven and earth will pass away, but My words will by no means pass away.
>
> —MATTHEW 24:35

> God is not a man, that He should lie, nor a son of man, that He should repent. Has He said, and will He not do? Or has He spoken, and will He not make it good?
>
> —NUMBERS 23:19

The words of Jesus penetrate the deepest recesses of the human heart. Peter, under the anointing of the Holy Spirit, having just come out of the Upper Room, preached to the multitude. "When they heard this, they were stung in the heart and said to Peter and to the rest of the apostles, 'Brothers, what shall we do?'" (Acts 2:37, MEV). Jesus told us that He would send the Holy Spirit, and "when He has come, He will convict the world of sin and of righteousness and of judgment" (John 16:8, MEV).

The words of Jesus expose every secret sin.

> In the beginning was the Word, and the Word was with God, and the Word was God....In Him was life, and the

life was the light of men. And the light shines in the darkness, and the darkness did not comprehend it.

—JOHN 1:1, 4–5

Jesus, who is the Word, is the Light of men. That Light exposes
all the secrets of the heart.

You have set our iniquities before You, our secret sins in
the light of Your countenance.

—PSALM 90:8

And have no fellowship with the unfruitful works of
darkness, but rather expose them. For it is shameful even
to speak of those things which are done by them in secret.
But all things that are exposed are made manifest by the
light, for whatever makes manifest is light.

—EPHESIANS 5:11–13

And not a creature exists that is concealed from His sight,
but all things are open and exposed, naked and defenseless to the eyes of Him with Whom we have to do.

—HEBREWS 4:13, AMPC

The words of Jesus execute judgment. When John saw a sword
coming from Jesus' mouth, he saw that the power of the words of
Jesus can subdue and overcome every enemy. He saw that God's
Word would judge all the nations of the earth.

Now out of His mouth goes a sharp sword, that with it He
should strike the nations.

—REVELATION 19:15

But with righteousness He shall judge the poor, and
decide with equity for the meek of the earth; He shall
strike the earth with the rod of His mouth, and with the
breath of His lips He shall slay the wicked.

—ISAIAH 11:4

Jesus was preparing a people for the most intense season the world would ever experience. He was constantly pointing to His real nature and what He was focused on, the end of the age. John saw this most powerful weapon, God's Word, proceeding from Jesus' mouth.

This image of Jesus striking the earth with the rod of His mouth is incredibly important. We live in a day when lies swirl all around us. It is easy to feel overwhelmed by the force of lying words flooding through media, entertainment, and social media platforms. It can seem like the message of the cross is buried under so many of the words of the cultural revolution. From political correctness to the assault on genders, the family, morality, and even the direct shaming of Christians, we can feel like we are losing. But as we focus on Jesus and the absolute power of His Word, we are greatly encouraged to stand strong.

The words of Jesus have supernatural and eternal power. Jesus does not speak to make you and me feel good. He declares the revelation of the nature and will of His Father so that we can be in agreement with Him. He is never afraid to hurt your feelings to get you to the truth. If you love truth and His Word, you will love the conviction that often comes when He speaks. You will ask Him for the sword of His mouth to cut through the confusion and deceptions of your heart.

Psalm 119 is one of my favorite psalms because the writers repeatedly cry out for God's judgment in their lives.

> With my lips I have declared all the judgments of Your mouth.
>
> —PSALM 119:13

> My soul breaks with longing for Your judgments at all times.
>
> —PSALM 119:20

> I have chosen the way of truth; Your judgments I have laid before me.
>
> —PSALM 119:30

Accept, I pray, the freewill offerings of my mouth, O
LORD, and teach me Your judgments.
—PSALM 119:108

Great are Your tender mercies, O LORD; revive me
according to Your judgments.
—PSALM 119:156

The entirety of Your word is truth, and every one of Your
righteous judgments endures forever.
—PSALM 119:160

Seven times a day I praise You, because of Your righteous
judgments.
—PSALM 119:164

Let my soul live, and it shall praise You; and let Your
judgments help me.
—PSALM 119:175

My heart's cry is for God to use the sword that comes from
His mouth to judge my heart that I might repent and come into
agreement with His Word. The judgments of God are a blessing to
those who love Him and yield to Him.

For the LORD will judge His people, and He will have
compassion on His servants.
—PSALM 135:14

The judgments of God that come from the sword proceeding out
of Jesus' mouth will bring life to the humble and wrath to the proud.

But the LORD shall endure forever; He has prepared His
throne for judgment. He shall judge the world in righteousness, and He shall administer judgment for the peoples in uprightness.
—PSALM 9:7–8

Rise up, O Judge of the earth; render punishment to the proud.

—PSALM 94:2

In June 1998 I had an incredible visitation. Two angels appeared to me while I was in my church building. One of the angels spoke to me and said, "Follow me. I have something to show you." He led me to the four corners of the church and showed me four angels that were coming to the earth to bring about a great restoration of the foundations of God's temple. I wrote a book about this called *Carriers of the Glory*.

I just want to mention a bit about the first angel. He was about nine feet tall and had a banner draped down his front. On the banner the word *Purity* was written. He had in his right hand a sword and in his left hand a shield. Both were made of the most amazing silver trimmed with gold that was so bright it was like fire. On the sword was the phrase *Word of God*, and on the shield I saw the word *Faith*.

The angel leading me spoke to me and said, "He has come to bring holiness back to the church. The sword has been given to pierce My people's hearts with the deepest of convictions, and the shield has been given to protect their minds from the vile thoughts of the enemy." A wave came from behind the angel called Purity and hit me. I trembled with the fear of God.

There is a release of the sword of the Lord coming first to the church and then to the world that will bring about the deepest convictions of the secret sins of the heart. This conviction is to be embraced by those who love God. He is sending His Word like a sword to remove from us everything that hinders love.

Prayer

Father, in the name of Your Son Jesus, teach me Your judgments. Pierce my heart with Your words of life. Expose the secret sins of my heart that I may confess and repent of them. I love Your Word and long to be conformed to Your image. Let the sword of the Lord remove everything from me that hinders my love relationship with Jesus. Amen.

Day 28
GOD'S WORD IS A SWORD, PART 2

Now out of His mouth goes a sharp sword,
that with it He should strike the nations.
—REVELATION 19:15

I CAN HARDLY BEGIN to comprehend how John felt while having this experience. The words and the vision were so overwhelming that he fell to the ground as dead. Imagine the power he must have been feeling as he saw the words of Jesus coming like a massive broadsword out of His mouth. Imagine the eternal living Word like a sword coming from One like the Son of Man, clothed in the priestly garment; His head and hair white; eyes burning with fiery, passionate desire; and holding the seven stars in His hand.

> Then I turned to see the voice that spoke with me. And having turned I saw seven golden lampstands, and in the midst of the seven lampstands One like the Son of Man, clothed with a garment down to the feet and girded about the chest with a golden band. His head and hair were white like wool, as white as snow, and His eyes like a flame of fire; His feet were like fine brass, as if refined in a furnace, and His voice as the sound of many waters; He had in His right hand seven stars, out of His mouth went a sharp two-edged sword, and His countenance was like the sun shining in its strength. And when I saw Him, I fell at His feet as dead.
> —REVELATION 1:12–17

Jesus was establishing in all of us that His Word has ultimate power over everything. Put that deep in your spirit. The Word of God is so powerful and penetrating that it judges and exposes the most secret thoughts and motives of the heart. Nothing can escape God's Word. Far too often we fail to see the truth that

God's Word always works. As a result, much of the church compromises, changes, waters down, or fails to speak the words of "thus saith the Lord."

Several years ago I went to a large inner-city church in Washington, DC. I was asked to speak to the teenagers at their Christian school. Actually, this was the private school where all the kids who got kicked out of public school went. These teens were not Christians for the most part. Gang members and drug dealers were in the crowd, as was every form of immorality. I showed up to preach dressed in a suit. The youth director told me to take off my tie. He said these kids were hard, inner-city kids who couldn't relate to a white guy in a suit.

I told him that he was about to see the greatest move of God that he had ever seen. I knew what was about to happen.

When I started preaching, the teachers and leaders stood along the wall with their arms folded and shook their heads in disapproval. They looked at each other like I was a fool as I preached about God's prophetic destiny on this young generation. I used many scriptures and spoke strong prophetic words.

When I gave the altar call for salvation, nearly all the teens came to the altar. Many started to cry, demons came out of others, and many were slain in the Spirit under the power of God. Many spoke in tongues for the first time. It was a Holy Ghost blowout. I handed the meeting back to the leaders, and later they came to me in utter disbelief. They said, "We thought you were a fool. We were sure these kids wouldn't respond to you. How did this happen?" I said, "You keep trying to speak to their minds, but I was preaching to their spirits."

I knew that the power of God's Word relates to every age, every race, every culture, and every socioeconomic level. The Word of God has supernatural power. The Word is to always be in our mouths. If we try to figure out how to soften God's Word for the unsaved and new Christians, we will fight against ourselves and God. We cannot improve on God's Word. We should not add to it nor take away from it. It is God's Word that exposes and transforms the human heart.

The Word of the Lord that is released in the days ahead is going to cut, convict, expose, and break through every stronghold and lie of the enemy. This intensified prophetic anointing will flood our mouths with the Word of God. It will be like a fire that consumes and like a hammer that breaks rocks into pieces.

> "Is not My word like a fire?" says the LORD, "And like a hammer that breaks the rock in pieces?"
> —JEREMIAH 23:29

Seeing this sword coming out of Jesus' mouth focuses us on the power and authority of every word that God speaks. It specifically draws our attention to the judgments of God and the fear of God. The fear of the Lord will keep you safe in the dangerous days that are upon us. Think about the mixture of the revelation John saw. He saw Jesus with eyes of fiery, passionate desire, and then he saw a mighty, powerful sword coming out of His mouth. John saw in visual form Proverbs 16:6: "By mercy and truth iniquity is purged; and by the fear of the LORD men depart from evil" (MEV).

The prophetic word of God is going to flood the earth. It will expose every lie and penetrate every heart. Men will be without excuse. This piercing word will first begin with the church. Many who slipped into the hyper-grace message will awaken. The spirit of holiness and deep conviction will return to the pulpits. Those who repent and yield to the Word of Jesus will see greater manifestations of God's power than they have ever seen before. Those who reject the Word and hold on to their false teachings will be judged.

> For the shepherds have become dull-hearted, and have not sought the LORD; therefore they shall not prosper, and all their flocks shall be scattered.
> —JEREMIAH 10:21

God requires His pastors and prophets to speak His Word, not enticing words that make people feel good.

> Therefore prepare yourself and arise, and speak to them
> all that I command you. Do not be dismayed before their
> faces, lest I dismay you before them.
>
> —JEREMIAH 1:17

The feel-good, hyper-grace, blessings-and-prosperity-without-struggle messages will fail. Instead, words of holiness, death to self, sacrificial love, and complete abandonment to Christ will fill the mouths of God's servants.

The true end-time prophets will arise and call the nations to repentance. They will be unafraid, unashamed, and fearless. They will not be concerned with being accepted by the multitudes but by being praised by the One. The only approval they will look for is the words, "Well done, thou good and faithful servant" (Matt. 25:21, KJV).

Jesus told us not to be afraid even when we are falsely accused, arrested, and persecuted. "But when they deliver you up, take no thought of how or what you will speak. For it will be given you at that time what you will speak. For it is not you who speak, but the Spirit of your Father who speaks through you" (Matt. 10:19–20, MEV).

Jesus' Word is a powerful sword. That Word in your mouth has supernatural power over all the power of the enemy. Satan wants to rob God's Word out of your mouth. He wants you to agree with and confess his lies. He wants you to feel like he is winning so there's no point in speaking up. Oh, dear child of God. Let God's Word fill your mouth. Speak with deep confidence that God's Word does not return void. God's Word will always produce what He sent it for. "So shall My word be that goes forth from My mouth; it shall not return to Me void, but it shall accomplish that which I please, and it shall prosper in the thing for which I sent it" (Isa. 55:11, MEV).

The command of the apostle Paul to Timothy applies to all of us.

> I charge [you] in the presence of God and of Christ Jesus,
> Who is to judge the living and the dead, and by (in the light
> of) His coming and His kingdom: Herald and preach the
> Word! Keep your sense of urgency [stand by, be at hand
> and ready], whether the opportunity seems to be favorable

or unfavorable. [Whether it is convenient or inconvenient, whether it is welcome or unwelcome, you as preacher of the Word are to show people in what way their lives are wrong.] And convince them, rebuking and correcting, warning and urging and encouraging them, being unflagging and inexhaustible in patience and teaching.

For the time is coming when [people] will not tolerate (endure) sound and wholesome instruction, but, having ears itching [for something pleasing and gratifying], they will gather to themselves one teacher after another to a considerable number, chosen to satisfy their own liking and to foster the errors they hold, and will turn aside from hearing the truth and wander off into myths and man-made fictions. As for you, be calm and cool and steady, accept and suffer unflinchingly every hardship, do the work of an evangelist, fully perform all the duties of your ministry.

—2 TIMOTHY 4:1–5, AMPC

When we see Jesus with a sharp two-edged sword coming out of His mouth, let us also see a sword coming out of our mouths as He speaks through us. In response to His Word in our mouths, some will repent and yield, and others will reject and seal their judgment. It is not your responsibility to get them to accept God's Word; it is your responsibility to speak the truth in love.

Prayer

Father, fill my mouth with Your words. The power that created the universe is in Your Word. Grant me the boldness to speak Your Word with confidence and love regardless of the circumstances. Cause Your words in my mouth to be spirit and life. I will fearlessly and faithfully declare Your words of truth from this day forward. In Jesus' holy name, amen.

Day 29

A FACE AS BRIGHT AS THE SUN

His countenance was like the sun shining in its strength.
—REVELATION 1:16

THE FOCUS HERE must be on Jesus' countenance, His face. When John saw Jesus' face shining like the sun, I can imagine that his mind was immediately flooded with memories of the transfiguration when he followed Christ up a high mountain along with Peter and James.

> Now after six days Jesus took Peter, James, and John his brother, led them up on a high mountain by themselves; and He was transfigured before them. His face shone like the sun, and His clothes became as white as the light.
> —MATTHEW 17:1–2

Yet this manifestation of Jesus' shining face seems to have been even more intense. John became overwhelmed and fell to the ground as though dead.

This brightness of Jesus' face is an expression of God's glory. There is much symbolism in this description that would take volumes to explore, but we will focus on one aspect. Beholding the beauty and majesty of Jesus' face shining in His brightness calls us into a transformative state. The brightness of the glory of God in the face of Jesus brings the greatest revelation of who He is into our hearts.

> For God Who said, Let light shine out of darkness, has shone in our hearts so as [to beam forth] the Light for the illumination of the knowledge of the majesty and glory of God [as it is manifest in the Person and is revealed] in the face of Jesus Christ (the Messiah).
> —2 CORINTHIANS 4:6, AMPC

God is calling us through this description to behold His glory as revealed in Jesus. I want you to put this deep into your spirit. There is coming upon the earth the greatest manifestation and demonstration of the glory of God, before the return of Christ, that the world has ever seen. These prophetic words have resonated in my heart for nearly thirty years.

God is about to release the brightness of His glory through the manifestation of the knowledge of Him as revealed in the face of Jesus. He has promised an end-time release of the glory of God upon His people.

> Arise, shine; for your light has come! And the glory of the LORD is risen upon you. For behold, the darkness shall cover the earth, and deep darkness the people; but the LORD will arise over you, and His glory will be seen upon you.
>
> —ISAIAH 60:1–2

This prophecy speaks of the glory of God on His people, the heavenly Jerusalem, the bride of Christ. This manifestation of His glory will be a corporate anointing that will shine for the world to see. This manifestation will bring about the harvest of souls.

> The Gentiles shall come to your light, and kings to the brightness of your rising. Lift up your eyes all around, and see: They all gather together, they come to you; your sons shall come from afar, and your daughters shall be nursed at your side. Then you shall see and become radiant, and your heart shall swell with joy; because the abundance of the sea shall be turned to you, the wealth of the Gentiles shall come to you.
>
> —ISAIAH 60:3–5

As the lost see the glory of God in the church, the multitudes will be converted. So what is this glory that is revealed in the brightness of Jesus' face?

We learn much by looking at Hebrew and Greek words for *glory.*

In the Hebrew the predominate word is *kabod*. It means "splendor, honor, respect, i.e., the attribution of high status to a person, wealth, i.e., what is valued and abundant, glorious presence, vast wealth, formally, wealth of riches, i.e., very extensive wealth and possessions."[1] It also describes a weight or heaviness, specifically, "heaviness, burden; riches; reputation, importance."[2]

In the Greek the word is *doxa*, which means "splendor, glory, brightness, shining, radiance, amazing might, demonstration of power."[3]

I like what my spiritual father, Dr. Morris Cerullo, said about the glory. He described glory as "all that God is and all that God has."[4] I find that simple definition quite good. The weightiness, glory, splendor, presence, wealth, and high status of God is truly "all that God is and all that God has." The glory speaks of the full manifestation of the totality of God.

His glory is not just a bright light or a cloud. It is the brightness that His essence produces. He is so pure, so true, so righteous, so all-powerful, all-knowing, and everywhere present that the brightness of His majesty is beyond human description. He is light itself.

To behold and experience His glory is to see God as He really is. It is far beyond a feeling, some goose bumps, or a few miracles. It is the brightness of His being and the manifestation of His fullness. We only see the smallest glimpse of it now, but we will see the fullness of it at the end of the age. The manifestation of the glory of God will increase exponentially until Jesus returns. The closer we are to the climax of the ages and the return of Jesus, the greater the manifestation of God's glory in and through the church will be experienced. This manifestation of the glory of God will produce the greatest transformation of the church into the image of Christ that has ever occurred.

Let's discover several things produced by the glory of God as revealed in the brightness of Jesus' face.

1. As we behold Him in His glory, we are changed into His image.

> And all of us, as with unveiled face, [because we] con-
> tinued to behold [in the Word of God] as in a mirror the
> glory of the Lord, are constantly being transfigured into
> His very own image in ever increasing splendor and from
> one degree of glory to another; [for this comes] from the
> Lord [Who is] the Spirit.
>
> —2 Corinthians 3:18, ampc

As we continue to behold God in His glory, we are changed from glory to glory. In other words, we are progressively transformed into His image as we behold Him in His glory. The more we see Him, the more we become like Him. No wonder the cry that God has put into the hearts of many is "show me Your glory."

2. It brings deliverance from every enemy.

> Restore us, O God of hosts; cause Your face to shine, and
> we shall be saved!
>
> —Psalm 80:7

So many Christians struggle with internal enemies more than external enemies. As we behold His glory in the face of Jesus, God arises, and every enemy inside and outside of us scatters.

> Let God arise, let His enemies be scattered; let those also
> who hate Him flee before Him. As smoke is driven away,
> so drive them away; as wax melts before the fire, so let
> the wicked perish at the presence of God.
>
> —Psalm 68:1–2

Although you can read this verse from a purely external enemy focus, I want you to consider this. All those thoughts, feelings, emotions, desires, and lusts inside of us that oppose God are His enemies. Those things of the flesh hate God. But as we behold Him in His glory and yield to His Spirit, those enemies scatter. Those wicked things in our hearts perish at the presence of God. Nothing transforms the human heart more than the revelation of the person of Jesus Christ.

3. The glory of God produces deep conviction of sin.

When Isaiah saw the glory of God in his vision in chapter 6, he was struck with deep conviction.

> Woe is me, for I am undone! Because I am a man of unclean lips, and I dwell in the midst of a people of unclean lips; for my eyes have seen the King, the LORD of hosts.
>
> —ISAIAH 6:5

Isaiah was a prophet of God, a man of God, yet when he saw the glory of God, he was deeply convicted. There are secret sins of our hearts that will only be exposed when faced with the brightness of the glory of God. Many false teachers say that the Holy Spirit would never convict a Christian of sin because Christians "can't sin." Oh, my dear friends. The greatest and deepest release of conviction that we have ever experienced will come when the glory is restored to the church. The Spirit of holiness will accompany the manifestation of God's glory and will cause conviction to pierce our hearts.

4. The glory of God produces the fear of the Lord.

> And the kings of the earth, the great men, the rich men, the commanders, the mighty men, every slave and every free man, hid themselves in the caves and in the rocks of the mountains, and said to the mountains and rocks, "Fall on us and hide us from the face of Him who sits on the throne and from the wrath of the Lamb! For the great day of His wrath has come, and who is able to stand?"
>
> —REVELATION 6:15–17

When the world sees the brightness of Jesus' face when He returns, they will tremble in fear because everything will be laid bare before His face. This fear of God will produce an awesome reverence and honor in people who yield to God and a terrifying dread of judgment in those who reject God.

5. The glory of God releases the judgments of God.

In his book *The Fear of the Lord*, John Bevere says, "The greater the glory, the greater the judgment."[5] He refers to the story when King David brought the ark of the covenant back to Jerusalem. When the ark reached the threshing floor, it stumbled, and Uzzah reached out his hand to steady it. When Uzzah irreverently touched the ark, God released judgment and Uzzah died. King David was distraught and angry with God until he realized that he had handled God's glory (the ark) incorrectly.

I was driving through my city of Corona, California, in the late 1990s asking God to send His glory to the churches. The Lord spoke to me and said, "I can't. If I send My glory, I will have to judge the churches, for the greater the glory, the greater the judgment." I understood that these churches were not ready to handle the heavy, weighty, glorious power of His manifested presence. They were too irreverent and treated the things of God too casually. If they were going to house God's glory, they would have to learn how to treat His presence with reverence.

> By those who come near Me I must be regarded as holy;
> and before all the people I must be glorified.
> —LEVITICUS 10:3

When we see Jesus' countenance shining like the sun, we fall on our knees in awe of Him. We gaze upon the beauty of His glory and are changed into His image. We want to reflect His glory to a lost and dying world. We become the reflection of Him in the earth until His return.

> Those who are wise shall shine like the brightness of the firmament, and those who turn many to righteousness like the stars forever and ever.
> —DANIEL 12:3

Prayer

Father, show me Your glory. I want to see You in the face of Jesus. I want to behold You in the beauty and majesty of all that You are and all that You possess. Let the light of Your countenance shine upon me. Open my eyes to behold You as You are, and transform me into Your image from glory to glory. In Jesus' holy name, amen.

Day 30
JESUS OUR SAVIOR

Do not be afraid; I am the First and the Last. I am He who lives, and was dead, and behold, I am alive forevermore. Amen. And I have the keys of Hades and of Death.

—REVELATION 1:17–18

W<small>E ARE NOW</small> at the final day of this incredible journey of looking unto Jesus. The amazing descriptions of Jesus in the first chapter of Revelation unveiled the key doctrines and truths of the gospel. John fell to the ground as one dead because of the impact of what he saw and heard.

Jesus reached out His hand and touched John. He then spoke these incredible words: "Do not be afraid." In these four simple words, Jesus tells us that no matter what we have seen of Him, or what He is about to show us is coming, we should not be afraid because He is *life* itself.

Jesus declared in Revelation 1:17, "I am He who lives, and was dead, and behold, I am alive forevermore." The best translation of the words "I am He who lives" is "I am the living One." This is an allusion to the covenant name for God, YHWH, which comes from the causative form of the Hebrew verb *to be*. (We see this usage in Exodus 3:14.) Jesus is the ever-living One.[1] Jesus is the One who is life itself. It is more than just that He is alive, but that He is *life*. He is the ever-eternal source of all life.

Then, in Revelation 1:18, Jesus makes an astounding statement: "I am He who lives, and was dead." Jesus, God Almighty, subjected Himself to death. He allowed Himself, the eternal God, to suffer death for us.

> For Christ also died for sins once for all, the just for the unjust, so that He might bring us to God, having been put to death in the flesh, but made alive in the spirit.
>
> —1 PETER 3:18, NASB

209

God died in the flesh. He experienced death for us.

> But we see Jesus, who was made a little lower than the
> angels, for the suffering of death crowned with glory and
> honor, that He, by the grace of God, might taste death for
> everyone.
>
> —HEBREWS 2:9

However, death could not hold Him, and the grave could not
contain Him. Jesus rose having conquered death. He defeated
death by coming back to life forevermore. The focus of the cross
is not that He died, but that He rose from the grave.

Jesus was telling us that we do not need to be afraid because He
already conquered death. He said in Revelation 1:18, "I have the
keys of Hades and of Death." Jesus took authority over death and
the grave once and for all.

> He will swallow up death forever, and the Lord GOD will
> wipe away tears from all faces.
>
> —ISAIAH 25:8

> God himself will be with them. He will wipe every tear
> from their eyes, and there will be no more death or sorrow
> or crying or pain. All these things are gone forever.
>
> —REVELATION 21:3–4, NLT

Jesus has total authority over death. Spiritual death has been
removed for those who are born again and whose names are
written in the Book of Life. They shall live forever even though
their natural bodies may die. No matter what happens to our natural bodies, we will live forever. This confidence gives us freedom
over the fear of dying.

> And do not fear those who kill the body but cannot kill
> the soul. But rather fear Him who is able to destroy both
> soul and body in hell.
>
> —MATTHEW 10:28

Freedom from the fear of death comes by focusing on our eternal life with Christ. God spoke to me a few years ago to prophetically tell His people, "Only a focus on eternity and the second coming of Christ will protect your minds from the onslaught of the enemy." The threats to our lives from governments, peoples, crises, famines, pestilences, economic chaos, and more are going to greatly increase. If we do not walk in the continual fresh revelation that Jesus conquered death, we will be overwhelmed and easily overcome.

Much of the church world is bound by fear. The recent years have proved this with the church's reaction to the COVID-19 pandemic. People were so afraid of dying that they fled the church, forsook one another, and did not care for the needy or elderly. Preachers hid behind a camera while their members suffered. Brother betrayed brother as pastors reported other pastors to the police because they decided to keep the church doors open and hold public services. All of this was driven by the fear of death.

God never *requested* for us to not fear. He *commanded* us to not fear. "Have not I commanded you? Be strong and courageous. Do not be afraid or dismayed, for the LORD your God is with you wherever you go" (Josh. 1:9, MEV).

Kenneth Copeland wrote this:

> The fear of death is the master fear that controls all other fear, and in today's world, people are overcome with fear of all sorts of things. But all fear comes down to the fear of death. If you find yourself in fear, all you need to do is renew your mind to the truth of God's Word, which says there is no fear in death when you are in Christ Jesus!... There is no fear in death because Jesus delivered us from death! Death no longer has victory over us (1 Corinthians 15:55), and the devil can't legitimately threaten us with death anymore. He has been defeated!
>
> But if we don't settle this issue, and if we aren't walking free from the law of sin and death, then the devil can use that against us to put us in bondage to the fear of death.[2]

All fear comes down to the fear of death. If you can conquer the fear of death, you can conquer all fear. Victory over the fear of death is in the resurrection. "Blessed be the God and Father of our Lord Jesus Christ, who according to His abundant mercy has given us a new birth into a living hope through the resurrection of Jesus Christ from the dead, to an incorruptible and undefiled inheritance that does not fade away, kept in heaven for you, who are protected by the power of God through faith for a salvation ready to be revealed in the last time" (1 Pet. 1:3–5, MEV).

The revelation of the resurrection delivers us from the fear of death. We can understand that we are forgiven of our sins through the shed blood of Jesus and as a result are delivered from the fear of judgment, yet still have the fear of death. But the fear of death is broken in the power of the resurrection. This is why a scripture from Romans 10 places two conditions on true salvation:

> That if you confess with your mouth the Lord Jesus and believe in your heart that God has raised Him from the dead, you will be saved.
>
> —ROMANS 10:9

Condition one: You make a covenant with your mouth that Jesus Christ has the legal right of authority over your life. (Confess with your mouth the Lord Jesus.)

Condition two: You put absolute trust in the fact that Jesus has conquered and gained total authority over death through His resurrection. (Believe in your heart that God has raised Him from the dead.)

Then you will be saved, not only from the judgment and consequences of sin but from the fear of death. This freedom from the fear of death is true freedom.

> For if we have been united together in the likeness of His death, certainly we also shall be in the likeness of His resurrection, knowing this, that our old man was crucified with Him, that the body of sin might be done away with, that we should no longer be slaves of sin. For he who has

died has been freed from sin. Now if we died with Christ,
we believe that we shall also live with Him, knowing that
Christ, having been raised from the dead, dies no more.
Death no longer has dominion over Him. For the death
that He died, He died to sin once for all; but the life that
He lives, He lives to God. Likewise you also, reckon your-
selves to be dead indeed to sin, but alive to God in Christ
Jesus our Lord.

—Romans 6:5–11

Finally, Jesus says, "I have the keys of Hades and of Death" (Rev.
1:18).

The keys speak of authority over something. Jesus is saying, "I
have total and absolute authority over death and the grave." He
did not just die on the cross to forgive our sins. He defeated death
and the grave, and He removed their threat over our lives forever.

Through this revelation Jesus is telling us to follow Him and
trust His voice because He has authority over death and the grave.
In John chapter 10 Jesus gives us the amazing illustration that He
is the Good Shepherd who lays down His life for His sheep.

For this reason the Father loves me, because I lay down
my life that I may take it up again. No one takes it from
me, but I lay it down of my own accord. I have authority
to lay it down, and I have authority to take it up again.
This charge I have received from my Father.

—John 10:17–18, esv

Because Jesus is *life* itself, He had the legal right to lay down
His life for us, and then the legal right to take it back through the
resurrection. He also has legal authority over death and the grave,
which He purchased through the shedding of His blood. Because
of His authority, we can live free from fear.

Jesus gives us the eternal guarantee that not even death can
take us away from Him. "My sheep hear my voice, and I know
them, and they follow me. I give them eternal life, and they will

never perish, and no one will snatch them out of my hand" (John 10:27–28, ESV).

Nothing can separate us from eternal life with Him. We need not fear, for God has said:

> If God is for us, who can be against us? He who did not spare His own Son, but delivered Him up for us all, how shall He not with Him also freely give us all things? Who shall bring a charge against God's elect? It is God who justifies. Who is he who condemns? It is Christ who died, and furthermore is also risen, who is even at the right hand of God, who also makes intercession for us. Who shall separate us from the love of Christ? Shall tribulation, or distress, or persecution, or famine, or nakedness, or peril, or sword? As it is written: "For Your sake we are killed all day long; we are accounted as sheep for the slaughter."
>
> Yet in all these things we are more than conquerors through Him who loved us. For I am persuaded that neither death nor life, nor angels nor principalities nor powers, nor things present nor things to come, nor height nor depth, nor any other created thing, shall be able to separate us from the love of God which is in Christ Jesus our Lord.
>
> —ROMANS 8:31–39

Nothing can separate us from our eternal life with God no matter how intense the circumstances of life are; no matter how much it seems like evil is winning; no matter what wicked governments do; no matter how violent the persecution becomes.

No matter how rejected by men you might feel, Jesus will never leave you or forsake you.

Prayer

Each day we have ended with a prayer. On this last day, I want you to go to the next and final chapter and pray the thirty declarations out loud. I encourage you to pray these declarations day after day and let them consume your heart and fill you with faith.

Conclusion
I SHALL OVERCOME

And when I saw Him, I fell at His feet as dead. But He laid His right hand on me, saying to me, "Do not be afraid."
—REVELATION 1:17

A T THE END of the first chapter of Revelation, Jesus reached down to John and touched Him. John had fallen to the ground as one dead, overwhelmed by the revelation he was seeing and hearing. Jesus then laid His hands on John and said, "Do not be afraid."

The revelation of Jesus will deliver you from fear. Jesus says to us, "Do not be afraid." Therefore, declare these out loud.

1. I will not fear because You are He who is, who was, and who is to come. You are the ever-eternal, ever-existing God. You fill the universe with Yourself and measure it with the span of Your hand.

2. I will not fear because You are He who has the seven Spirits. You give me the seven manifestations of the Holy Spirit that will give to me all the power, wisdom, and knowledge I need to overcome.

3. I will not fear because You are Jesus, the name that is above every name. You do all things for Your name's sake and for Your glory. All authority has been given to You.

4. I will not fear because You are Christ the Messiah. You brought good news of the kingdom of heaven to the poor, freedom from oppression, and healing for my broken heart.

5. I will not fear because You are the faithful witness. You were faithful, even unto death, to fulfill the will of the Father. Therefore, You are worthy of my complete trust.

6. I will not fear because You are the firstborn from the dead. You live in a resurrected body, fully God and fully man. When I see You, I shall be like You.

7. I will not fear because You are the ruler of the kings of the earth. You have all authority in heaven and in earth. You are coming back to take complete control of the kingdoms of this world, and we, Your people, shall rule and reign with You.

8. I will not fear because You are the One who loves us and washed us in Your blood. We were created to be Your bride. We are the Father's gift to You. You have come to rescue Your bride from everything that hinders love.

9. I will not fear because You have made us a kingdom of priests. We are joint heirs with You as priests of the Father exercising His power and authority on the earth.

10. I will not fear because You are coming with the clouds. You shall return riding on the clouds of glory produced by the prophetic prayers and worship of Your people.

11. I will not fear because You are the God of patience. In the midst of my afflictions You release Your supernatural ability to patiently endure until the end.

12. I will not fear because You are He who has the voice like a trumpet. You are calling me up to

where You are and will prophetically reveal to me
the secrets of Your plan, Your purpose, and Your
will. I will hear Your voice and not go astray.

13. I will not fear because You are the Alpha. You are
preeminent above all things. You are the beginning
of all creation. All things exist through You.

14. I will not fear because You are the Omega. You
have the final say over everything. You are the capstone. You are returning, and our reward is with
You.

15. I will not fear because You are the First. You, being
God, became man, so I can fully engage with You
intimately.

16. I will not fear because You are the Last. You have
defeated forever everything that hinders Your love.

17. I will not fear because You are in the midst of the
lampstands. You will build Your church, and the
gates of hell will not prevail against it. The church
is Your bride and shall be one flesh with You for
eternity.

18. I will not fear because You are the Son of Man. You
shared in all my weaknesses yet overcame them so
that I too can overcome. You merged God and man
forever, and You will rule and reign forever.

19. I will not fear because You are He who is clothed
with a priestly garment. You have covered me with
purity by Your blood, consecrated me, and separated me from the world, so as I remain in You, I
can come to the holy of holies.

20. I will not fear because You are He who has the golden band around Your chest. You exercise abso- lute authority as High Priest. You reconciled me to the Father, and You live to intercede for me.

21. I will not fear because You are He whose head and hair are white like snow. You have perfect wisdom to lead and guide me through every aspect of my life. I can completely trust Your leadership.

22. I will not fear because You are He who has eyes like flames of fire. You burn with fiery, passionate desire for me. You are jealous for my heart and affections. You see all. Nothing is hidden from Your sight, and You will judge the wicked.

23. I will not fear because Your feet are as brass. You are the God of perfect justice and judgment. You bore our judgment on the cross and will judge the wicked at the end of the age.

24. I will not fear because Your voice is the sound of many waters. Your voice is musical and is releasing an end-time prophetic prayer and wor- ship anointing. I am a prayer partner with You in releasing the kingdom of heaven into the earth.

25. I will not fear because You hold seven stars in Your right hand. You have anointed and appointed Your leaders and have given them grace gifts to help me mature. You have Your leaders in Your right hand. I can fully trust You.

26. I will not fear because You have a two-edged sword proceeding from Your mouth. Your Word is eternal

and will never fail. Nothing can stop the power of Your prophetic word spoken through my mouth.

27. I will not fear because You are He whose countenance is like the sun. The brightness of Your glory is coming back to the church before You come for the church. The favor of Your countenance shines upon me.

28. I will not fear because You are He who lives. You are life itself. In You, I have abundant life. Because You live, I too shall live eternally.

29. I will not fear because You are He who was dead and is alive forevermore. You tasted death for us all and conquered it through Your resurrection. At the last trumpet I too shall be resurrected. I will receive my heavenly body and be with You forever.

30. I will not fear because You are He who has the keys of hades and death. You have defeated the grave and have given me eternal life. Therefore, I need not fear. Death has no hold on me.

But now, thus says the LORD, who created you, O Jacob, and He who formed you, O Israel: "Fear not, for I have redeemed you; I have called you by your name; you are Mine. When you pass through the waters, I will be with you; and through the rivers, they shall not overflow you. When you walk through the fire, you shall not be burned, nor shall the flame scorch you. For I am the LORD your God, the Holy One of Israel, your Savior."

—ISAIAH 43:1–3

Fear not. The days may be evil, the circumstances difficult, the persecutions increasing, and the battles abounding, but we are "looking unto Jesus, the author and finisher of our faith, who for the joy that was set before Him endured the cross, despising the shame, and has sat down at the right hand of the throne of God" (Heb. 12:2).

Jesus is telling us in this day: "Behold, I am coming quickly! Hold fast what you have, that no one may take your crown. He who overcomes, I will make him a pillar in the temple of My God, and he shall go out no more" (Rev. 3:11–12).

> These things I have spoken to you, that in Me you may have peace. In the world you will have tribulation; but be of good cheer, I have overcome the world.
>
> —John 16:33

> And this is the victory that has overcome the world—our faith.
>
> —1 John 5:4

> So then faith comes by hearing, and hearing by the word of God.
>
> —Romans 10:17

Nothing transforms the human heart like the ever-increasing revelation of the person of Jesus Christ. As we see Jesus in the Word of God, we shall be filled with His faith and power to overcome the world. For He has said, "No weapon that is formed against you shall prosper, and every tongue that shall rise against you in judgment, you shall condemn. This is the heritage of the servants of the Lord" (Isa. 54:17, MEV).

Looking Unto Jesus: 30 Days of Transformation is just the beginning. As we continue to behold Him, we will be transformed into His image from glory to glory. He says, "It is given to you to know the mysteries of the kingdom of heaven" (Matt. 13:11, MEV).

We may be concluding this book, but we are only beginning this journey of the revelation of Jesus Christ. Let Philippians 3:10 be your heart's cry.

[For my determined purpose is] that I may know Him [that I may progressively become more deeply and intimately acquainted with Him, perceiving and recognizing and understanding the wonders of His Person more strongly and more clearly], and that I may in that same way come to know the power outflowing from His resurrection [which it exerts over believers], and that I may so share His sufferings as to be continually transformed [in spirit into His likeness even] to His death.

—PHILIPPIANS 3:10, AMPC

NOTES

DAY 1

1. Blue Letter Bible, s.v. *"eirēnē,"* accessed October 18, 2022, https://www. blueletterbible.org/lexicon/g1515/kjv/tr/0-1/.
2. Rick Brannan, ed., *Lexham Research Lexicon of the Hebrew Bible* (Bellingham, WA: Lexham Press, 2020).

DAY 2

1. Robert Jamieson, A. R. Fausset, and David Brown, *Commentary Critical and Explanatory on the Whole Bible* (Bellingham, WA: Faithlife, 1997), Revelation 5:6.
2. Jamieson, Fausset, and Brown, *Commentary Critical and Explanatory on the Whole Bible*, Revelation 5:6.
3. Francis Brown, S. R. Driver, and Charles Briggs, *The Abridged Brown-Driver-Briggs Hebrew-English Lexicon of the Old Testament*, ed. Richard Whitaker (Boston: Houghton Mifflin, 1906).
4. James A. Swanson, *Dictionary of Biblical Languages With Semantic Domains: Hebrew (Old Testament)* (Bellingham, WA: Faithlife, 1997).
5. Swanson, *Dictionary of Biblical Languages With Semantic Domains: Hebrew (Old Testament)*.
6. Swanson, *Dictionary of Biblical Languages With Semantic Domains: Hebrew (Old Testament)*.
7. Swanson, *Dictionary of Biblical Languages With Semantic Domains: Hebrew (Old Testament)*.
8. Swanson, *Dictionary of Biblical Languages With Semantic Domains: Hebrew (Old Testament)*.
9. Brannan, *Lexham Research Lexicon of the Hebrew Bible*.

DAY 3

1. "Yeshua: The Jewish Word for Salvation," Jews for Jesus, December 1, 1987, https://jewsforjesus.org/publications/newsletter/newsletter-dec-1987/y-shua-the-jewish-word-for-salvation/.

DAY 4

1. Robert L. Thomas, *New American Standard Hebrew-Aramaic and Greek Dictionaries: Updated Edition* (Foundation Publications, 1998).
2. Benjamin S. Davis, "Poverty," in Douglas Mangum, Derek R. Brown, Rachel Klippenstein, and Rebekah Hurst, eds., *Lexham Theological Wordbook* (Bellingham, WA: Lexham Press, 2014).
3. Thomas, *New American Standard Hebrew-Aramaic and Greek Dictionaries: Updated Edition*.
4. "Forgiveness: Your Health Depends on It," Johns Hopkins Medicine, accessed October 18, 2022, https://www.hopkinsmedicine.org/health/wellness-and-prevention/forgiveness-your-health-depends-on-it.

5. James A. Swanson, *Dictionary of Biblical Languages With Semantic Domains: Greek (New Testament)* (Bellingham, WA: Faithlife, 1997).

DAY 5

1. Swanson, *Dictionary of Biblical Languages With Semantic Domains: Greek (New Testament)*.
2. Swanson, *Dictionary of Biblical Languages With Semantic Domains: Greek (New Testament)*.
3. Swanson, *Dictionary of Biblical Languages With Semantic Domains: Hebrew (Old Testament)*.

DAY 8

1. Steve Foss, *Satan's Big Fat Lie* (Lake Mary, FL: Charisma House, 2022), 153.

DAY 9

1. Jamieson, Fausset, and Brown, *Commentary Critical and Explanatory on the Whole Bible*, Revelation 1:6.
2. Zachary Garris, "The Levites—A Class of Warrior-Priests," Knowing Scripture, April 17, 2018, https://knowingscripture.com/articles/levites-class-of-warrior-priests.

DAY 11

1. Thomas, *New American Standard Hebrew-Aramaic and Greek Dictionaries: Updated Edition*.
2. Martin Vincent, *Vincent's Word Studies in the New Testament*, vol. 1 (New York: Charles Scribner's Sons, 1887), 679.

DAY 12

1. Dr. David Cooper, "Rules of Interpretation: The Law of First Mention," Biblical Research Society, accessed October 18, 2022, https://www.biblicalresearch.info/page48.html.

DAY 13

1. Wikipedia, s.v. "Alpha," accessed October 18, 2022, https://en.wikipedia.org/wiki/Alpha.
2. *Merriam-Webster*, s.v. "omega," accessed October 18, 2022, https://www.merriam-webster.com/dictionary/omega.
3. Mike Bickle, "Jesus, Our Magnificent Obsession, Part 2," IHOPKC, February 10, 2012, https://backup.storage.sardius.media/file/akamaiBackup-ihopkc-103762/IHOP/680/107/20120210-T-Jesus_as_the_Alpha_and_Omega_JOM03.pdf.
4. Bickle, "Jesus, Our Magnificent Obsession, Part 2."
5. Swanson, *Dictionary of Biblical Languages With Semantic Domains: Hebrew (Old Testament)*.

DAY 14

1. Martin Vincent, *Word Studies in the New Testament*, vol. 2 (New York: Charles Scribner's Sons, 1887), 432.

DAY 15

1. Jamieson, Fausset, and Brown, *Commentary Critical and Explanatory on the Whole Bible*, Revelation 1:12.
2. "Gates of Hell," That the World May Know With Ray Vander Laan, accessed October 18, 2022, https://www.thattheworldmayknow.com/gates-of-hell-article.

DAY 18

1. Thomas, *New American Standard Hebrew-Aramaic and Greek Dictionaries: Updated Edition.*

DAY 19

1. Swanson, *Dictionary of Biblical Languages With Semantic Domains: Hebrew (Old Testament).*
2. Brannan, *Lexham Research Lexicon of the Hebrew Bible.*
3. Vincent, *Word Studies in the New Testament*, vol. 2, 317.

DAY 20

1. Swanson, *Dictionary of Biblical Languages With Semantic Domains: Greek (New Testament).*
2. Swanson, *Dictionary of Biblical Languages With Semantic Domains: Greek (New Testament).*

DAY 22

1. Brannan, *Lexham Research Lexicon of the Hebrew Bible.*
2. Jamieson, Fausset, and Brown, *Commentary Critical and Explanatory on the Whole Bible*, Song of Solomon 4:6.

DAY 26

1. Swanson, *Dictionary of Biblical Languages With Semantic Domains: Hebrew (Old Testament).*
2. Brannan, *Lexham Research Lexicon of the Hebrew Bible.*
3. Swanson, *Dictionary of Biblical Languages With Semantic Domains: Hebrew (Old Testament).*
4. Swanson, *Dictionary of Biblical Languages With Semantic Domains: Hebrew (Old Testament).*
5. Swanson, *Dictionary of Biblical Languages With Semantic Domains: Hebrew (Old Testament).*

DAY 27

1. Vincent, *Word Studies in the New Testament*, vol. 1, 276.

DAY 29

1. Swanson, *Dictionary of Biblical Languages With Semantic Domains: Hebrew (Old Testament)*.
2. Brannan, *Lexham Research Lexicon of the Hebrew Bible*.
3. Swanson, *Dictionary of Biblical Languages With Semantic Domains: Greek (New Testament)*.
4. Dr. Morris Cerullo, 1987 Unity of the Spirit conference.
5. John Bevere, *The Fear of the Lord* (Lake Mary, FL: Charisma House, 2006).

DAY 30

1. Bob Utley, *Hope in Hard Times—The Final Curtain: Revelation* (Marshall, TX: Bible Lessons International, 2001), 26.
2. Kenneth Copeland, "There Is No Fear in Death—Ministry Minute With Kenneth Copeland," Kenneth Copeland Ministries, January 31, 2018, https://blog.kcm.org/no-fear-ministry-minute-kenneth-copeland/.